MY MOTHER'S WAR

A Holocaust Survivor's Tribute
To An Extraordinary Woman

Michael Fryd

MY MOTHER'S WAR

A Holocaust Survivor's Tribute
To An Extraordinary Woman

Michael Fryd

Story
Sanctum
PUBLISHING

Cover photos provided by Michael Fryd and National Archives (Public Domain: German Troops March Through Warsaw by Jger Hugo, 1939 (NARA).

Cover design and interior formatting by Casselberry Creative Design.

This book is memoir. It reflects the author's present recollections of experiences over time. Some names and characteristics have been changed, some events have been compressed, and some dialogue has been recreated.

Story Sanctum Publishing
First Edition

ISBN: 979-8-9886653-0-4

Dedication

to Marc and Kim

TABLE OF CONTENTS

PREFACE

I wrote this memoir to share my experiences and memories of the Holocaust with my American-born children who grew up safe and comfortable in the United States. I hoped it would help them connect to the large family they never met and a long-gone tradition.

I wasn't sure how the story would develop but didn't want another Holocaust tale of woe describing human cruelty in gory detail. Continuous repetition of indescribable atrocities numbs our souls, reduces the Holocaust to an abstract historical event that one can study, analyze, and intellectualize; an event discussed in generalities: six million Jews, Roma, people with mental disabilities, and members of the LGBTQ community targeted and killed. This allows us to avoid coming face to face with the pain and fear felt by each individual who had the rotten luck of being the wrong person, in the wrong place, at the wrong time.

I chose instead to focus on my family's experiences, write about our victory because each Jew who survived the Holocaust represented a victory over the Haman of our generation. I didn't avoid noting the horrors that occurred around us, but wanted them to be secondary, a background against which we struggled to survive.

While writing, I realized the heart of the story was my larger-than-life mother, Evelyn Fryd. We survived against all odds because the Nazis and Polish anti-Semites were no match for her. During those years she was a mythic figure, endowed with boundless energy and cunning, determined to do whatever it took to save her family from Hitler's clutches. She deserved the title "A Woman of Valor" inscribed on her tomb. However, it is the second inscription, "A Survivor of the Holocaust," that defined and crippled her for the rest of her life. This was the invisible war wound that festered and wouldn't heal. She never learned to stop being a survivor; spent her life accumulating a war chest, preparing for the next "Holocaust." Even after half a lifetime in the United States, she never felt safe. The great tragedy of her life was she couldn't turn off her survival skills even when they were not just unnecessary but bordered on sociopathic; she had to outsmart and outmaneuver everyone, even those she loved. She had to win every encounter, be sharper, quicker, more cunning, because anything less was too dangerous.

I included a bit of family history, the times and places that shaped my parents and made their worldview so different. I divided the memoir into five parts: the first describes my parents' life in Poland before World War II, their struggles to set up a middle-class life in a small Polish town, the second covers the war years after the German invasion of Poland, years spent first as prisoners in a ghetto, followed by three years hiding out in a farm's root cellar. The final three parts describe our life after liberation as we flee the killing fields of Poland to Paris and finally New York.

That last period was almost as difficult as the war years. My parents, who had lost everything, had to rebuild their life in a world that expected them to behave as if nothing happened and to follow the rules of civilized society when that same society had treated them with such a lack of civility.

PART ONE

The Pre-War Years

1

MY FATHER'S FAMILY

Being a Jew in Poland was always problematic. We were a convenient scapegoat for whatever ailed the local populace, but my birth year, 1936, was more inauspicious than most. It marked the start of Nazi expansionist moves that led to the slaughter of three million Polish Jews.

I entered the world at 17 Koscielna ulica (Church Street) in Wolomin, a small town twenty miles from Warsaw. Koscielna ulica was the main drag connecting the two focal points of every small Polish town I ever saw: the marketplace and the railroad station. The church, catholic with a capital C, dominated the marketplace as it did everything else in our town and the rest of Poland. The marketplace was busiest on Thursdays when farmers came to town to sell their produce. Peddlers hawking clothes, pots and pans, notions, and other assorted wares followed them. In many villages, farmers and peddlers celebrated the end of market day by indulging in the weekly cultural highlight, getting drunk after consuming gargantuan quantities of the national brew, vodka.

I realize how sarcastic and condescending these words sound, but what often followed the drinking in small rural villages colors my bitterness towards Poles. Fueled by an excess of 100 proof alcohol, farmers indulged in another favorite national pastime, blaming the Żydy (Jews) for poor crops, cows not giving milk, high taxes, the general decline in national morality, and anything else that came to mind. Filled with righteous indignation, they set out in search of "bastard Christ killers." Often, they would just pass out exhausted after breaking a few windows and pulling a few beards, but every once in a while, things escalated into a full-scale mini pogrom. They burned houses, raped Jewish women, beat up, and sometimes killed Jewish men. The police seldom found or punished the perpetrators. However, they had better luck arresting and convicting Jews who harmed the attackers.

I remember my father telling me what happened in his village when the local Jews, tired of being victims, imported a few "shtarkers" (Jewish tough guys) from Warsaw to protect them. The peasants out to have some fun met their match that night. Instead of cowering villagers, they encountered seasoned street fighters who beat the crap out of them. The police arrested the defenders and charged them with an unprovoked attack on innocent farmers. The court sentenced them to long jail sentences and throughout Poland, newspaper headlines decried this latest outrage perpetrated by "the evil descendants of the Pharisees."

But I digress, I was born at home in the back of my parents' sporting goods, bicycle, and radio shop. Our living quarters comprised a sizeable living room and a small kitchen half filled by a huge wood burning cooking stove. Water came from a hand-cranked pump in the backyard, which was also the site of a wooden outhouse. My parents spent their free time in the living room; we ate our meals there, entertained guests, and in my case stayed in whatever enclosure, highchair or crib they placed me. The Baginskis, an old Polish couple who sold the house to my parents, occupied the second floor. We slept in two rooms on the second floor of a red brick two-story apartment building next door. Our backyard was long and narrow, with rows of vegetables growing in the back, and a veritable jungle of bushes on the right-hand side of the house.

My parents, an odd, mismatched couple, wound up married and owning this store in Wolomin through a series of improbable turns of fortune. My father was the youngest of Moishe and Rachel Fryd's eleven surviving children. She had six miscarriages. Grandpa Moishe, my namesake, and grandma Rachel became husband and wife through an arranged marriage, which was customary in their time. They didn't meet until their wedding day; she was fourteen and he, fifteen. After the ceremony, following the Orthodox tradition, they shaved her head and made her put on a wig. Rachel told my mother, years later, how unready she was to become a wife, never mind an adult. After the ceremony, the child bride went out in the yard and, while everyone else was celebrating, used her wig as a sand bucket to make mud pies. Still, a year later, she gave birth to my aunt Rivkah, who made her a grandmother by the time she was just past thirty.

Following custom, they lived with Rachel's parents for several years. The number of years a bride's parents supported a newlywed couple was often part of the dowry. The size of the dowry, after considering the bride's family's wealth, depended on the relative attractiveness of the bride and groom. They measured attractiveness by criteria you may find bizarre and archaic, but they reflected the values and needs of the Jewish community in Poland. The overriding criterion for both sides was the families' reputation for religiosity, honesty, and learning.

A groom's most desirable attribute was his promise as a Torah scholar; all other knowledge was inconsequential and even suspect, a sign of potential assimilation. Mathematics was the major exception. It was useful in commerce and the intricate study of the Kabbalah.

Therefore, excessive pallor, an undernourished physique, and stooped shoulders, indicative of a life spent indoors bent over learned books while neglecting physical needs, were that time's equivalent of a well-defined six-pack. An attractive girl was healthy, capable of bearing children, and an excellent housekeeper. Wealth was a plus, although parents tried to arrange marriages with families within the same economic class. Sometimes, a rich family would accept a poor son-in-law if he showed exceptional promise as a scholar who would raise their social status when he became, as expected, a learned rabbi, or if their daughter was a cripple or mentally challenged.

Cultural anthropological footnotes aside, after seven years, grandpa Moishe used the hard cash part of the dowry to buy a farm in the village of Prostyn and rented out the fields to Polish farmers. He did some logging on his land, set up a fish farm, and bought and sold land. He was prosperous for many years and became known in the area as Moishe Prostyner. This was a sign of respect and status that of all the Moishes in the village, he was THE Moishe and given the village's name as an identifying surname.

However, despite his wealth and lofty social status, Moishe had problems and disappointments; he had too many daughters who would require dowries, and his first four sons showed no aptitude for Torah scholarship. One can imagine his joy when his youngest child, my father, born to Moishe and Rachel when they were almost fifty, showed signs of precocious intelligence. Moishe decided his little genius would become a rabbi and bring koved (glory and status) to the family.

The path to scholarly learning and ultimate theological glory exposed my father to years of brutality, hunger, fear, and loneliness. At age five, the spoiled and fawned upon family baby, left home to study, and live with a melamed (a teacher of Torah). There, along with several other Wunderkinder, he spent thirteen years in a dirty chilly room, which served as both classroom and dormitory, learning to memorize scholastic debates by ancient sages, intended to explain obscure passages in the Torah. The melamed, a scholar manqué, was a tyrannical pedant whose main pedagogical tool was a stick he plied with religious fervor upon the head and back of any unfortunate who showed an occasional memory lapse, lack of interest, or worst of all any signs of independent thought or originality. These latter two crimes were the most heinous, since everyone knew that any deviation from tradition or questioning of authority was evidence of incipient assimilation. Any self-respecting teacher had to exorcise such demonic tendencies by smiting the offending student with all his might, even if in the process the heretic suffered serious physical harm. No melamed wanted another "apikoros" (Epicurean), another Spinosa in his school.

The boys ate bread and coffee in the morning and a piece of bread for lunch. Jewish families in town provided dinner for the young scholars. They treated the boys like beggars and fed them leftovers. My father told me he was always hungry, too afraid to ask the melamed for another piece of bread and too ashamed to ask his resentful dinner hosts for more food. I suspect his obsessive focus on food in later years resulted from this scarring experience.

He saw his family only twice a year when he went home for the high holidays and Passover. No matter how miserable, he couldn't tell his parents he wanted to quit; it wasn't his decision to make. He could see his father kvell (swell with pride) when he recited, for family friends, arcane passages from the Torah along with the accompanying arguments and commentaries by the great sages such as Raschi or Maimonides. Grandpa Moishe had grand dreams for his youngest child. He was his last chance to raise the family's scholarly reputation. In those days, patriarchs ruled with an iron fist, and my father and grandma Rachel hinted Moishe was more tyrannical than most. He wouldn't allow childish whining to derail his dreams.

Despite the rigors of his student days, my father survived and was almost ready for ordination as a rabbi when the Tsar intervened. He was almost 18, World War I was still on when kicking and screaming he became a soldier in the Russian army. His miserable life at the Yeshiva looked warm and appealing compared to the hell awaiting the young rabbinical student, complete with ear locks, beard, and Hasidic garb, in this hotbed of anti-Semitism. The closest approximation to his unfortunate situation would be a black college student thrown in with a platoon of bubbas from the Mississippi branch of the Aryan nation. They bullied him, with no one to defend or protect him, since the officers and noncoms were just as prejudiced.

Like at the Yeshiva, he was always hungry; he couldn't eat most army food because it wasn't kosher, and his "buddies" stole any packages from home. He survived for months on bread, water, and an occasional boiled potato. It is a measure of the survival skills he gained at the Yeshiva that he overcame the prejudice and harassment and over time even prospered. He became a corporal, an unheard-of thing for a Jew, and a star winger on his regimental soccer team. "I was very short," he told me, "but quick; I could always outrun those big farm boys."

The army didn't kill him, but it changed him. The man who emerged four years later was not the boy who entered it. While still religious, he was not a Hasid anymore and had no intentions of becoming a rabbi. This was one more hideous blow to grandpa Moishe, who, during my father's time in the army, fell on hard times.

The prevailing belief of the times was that even a righteous Jew couldn't enter heaven if he hadn't met his obligations on earth by marrying off all his daughters. By the time my father came home from the army, Moishe sold most of his land to provide for six dowries and lived off support checks sent from America by his oldest daughter Rivkah, who had a thriving clothing business in Hazelton, Pennsylvania.

Moishe was furious with his wayward son, refused to buy him any clothes other than the traditional Hasidic garb, or help him get a job.

He raised a rabbi and would settle for nothing less. For years, he'd dreamt his son would become a scholar, a light unto Israel, and he couldn't give up the dream. What scared him most was the possibility this refusal to continue rabbinical studies was just the first symptom of assimilation.

My father hung around the farm for several months, wore his military clothes, became bored, depressed, but unrepentant. He had nothing to do, no prospects, subjected to unremitting pressure and disapproval from his disappointed sire. His unhappy stay on the farm ended when Moishe's worst fears came true. An acquaintance in an adjoining village spilled the beans. He saw my father play soccer for a local gentile team the previous Saturday. The thought his son, predestined to be a rabbi, spent the Sabbath running around in short pants, *OY! Bareheaded, OY VEY! With a bunch of goyim, OY VEY IS MEER!* was more than he could handle. When my father came home from the next game, he found the door locked and his few belongings in an old valise on the now unwelcome mat.

With no money and no skills, other than playing soccer and an extensive knowledge of the Torah, the only job he could get was with an older widowed cousin who owned a hardware store in Wolomin. She gave him room and board and very little else, in return for helping her run the shop and providing (reluctantly he assured me) other services of a more intimate nature. It was this latter activity that forced him to leave her employ. The widow decided after a while they should marry and legitimize their relationship. However, while he was grudgingly willing to be a boy toy, an image that blew my mind, he was no more ready to become her husband than he was to become a rabbi.

Kicked out once again for refusing to assume a role thrust upon him by someone else's wishes, he became a traveling agent for Singer sewing machines. He went from farm to farm, peddling sewing machines to farmers' wives and daughters. Blessed with a gift of gab, he became quite a charmer with the ladies, which helped raise both his sales and satiate his libido. I found it hard to visualize the fussy old man I knew as a rake, but I have it on good authority he had to keep changing sales territories to escape angry farmers intent on providing him with a total circumcision.

But it wasn't all just fun and games; he wanted to make money, become independent, and never again have to rely on someone else's goodwill. He started buying the machines wholesale from Singer and selling them on an installment plan, earning both a commission for the sale and interest on the loan. After a while, tired of life on the road, he used the capital he'd accumulated to buy the house on Koscielna ulica and open a bicycle shop. At thirty, he was an affluent, charming bachelor with an active social life, and a respected member of the local Jewish community.

His father died two years earlier and didn't witness his success, but Grandma Rachel was still alive, and eager to see her baby married. Society viewed thirty-year-old unmarried men as abnormal, an embarrassment to their family. He withstood the family pressures until his pursuit of mental, rather than carnal, stimulation got him into trouble.

Wolomin, like most small suburbs, both now and then, was not a hotbed of sophistication. The few literate souls in town met often for tea and philosophical discussions. They debated long into the night the relative merits of socialism versus communism, Trotskyism versus Stalinism, but agreed, in principle, on the need for a social revolution. This harmless group of parlor revolutionaries scaled no barricades other than those separating them from the tea and strudel, but the Polish government at the time was going through a McCarthyite phase of its own, determined to crush any potential communist cells before they got started. My father, alerted by a friend on the police force, left town for a few months to avoid arrest and let things cool down. Reluctant to stay with his mother, he hid out with his oldest brother,

Motcheh Mendel, who lived in Pultusk next door to my future grandparents.

2

My Mother's Family

My mother's father, Mendel Brzoza, had been a specialty printer in the town of Prushnitz. He may have been a lithographer. I remember my mother commenting on how strong he was: he could lift the very heavy stone plates used for printing by himself. He sounded prosperous and had five children with his first wife, who died when he was close to sixty.

His children married and out of the house, he lived alone but didn't relish a single lifestyle. He married Rana Goldberg, a much younger woman, a victim of arranged marriages' hidden problems. Rana's parents married her off as a teenager to a boy from an excellent family. They spent a lot of time checking out the character and reputation of the groom's family, but they never inquired into his interest in or attraction to the opposite sex. After a few years of a loveless marriage, Rana got a divorce. However, through no fault of her own, she'd become damaged goods and had to choose from a pool of other blemished marital prospects.

I can't believe that Mendel, old enough to be her grandfather, was the least objectionable of the lot. But at least his five children bore evidence of his willingness to engage women on a physical level. While Mendel was eager to remarry, his grown children were bitter. They saw the brief interval between marriages, only a few months after her death, as an affront to their mother's memory, and refused to accept a stepmother younger than themselves. Those feelings persisted. I remember my mother complaining that her half brothers and sisters, all affluent, wouldn't help her family even when they were on the edge of starvation.

My mother, Evelyn, the fourth of Mendel and Rana's five children, was born in Pultusk where her parents resettled after a rather bloody pogrom in Prushnitz. I don't know why Mendel wasn't able to work as a printer in Pultusk, but I gathered from my mother that they found it difficult to make ends meet on the paltry income he made from doing odd jobs. They supplemented this with vegetables they grew in the backyard, eggs from a few hens and milk from two goats. They kept the goats in the basement, out of the yard because the miserable creatures would decimate the garden. The family fed them potato peels my mother collected every day by going house to house, begging people for the privilege of going through their garbage.

The goats almost caused Mendel's death. One Thursday, a young Polish boy, tired from running around the marketplace, fell asleep in the hay on a farmer's wagon. When the market closed, the farmer, having sold all his produce, returned home unaware of the boy's presence. When he discovered the unwitting hitchhiker, he waited till the next market day to return him; he didn't want to waste a day going back to Pultusk. In the meantime, the frantic parents were turning the town upside down. After a few days, everyone assumed he was dead, and since it was a few days before Passover, killed by Jews who, as everyone believed, needed a young child's blood to make matzos. This vile fantasy accepted as fact throughout Poland was one more excuse for hating Jews.

A townie remembered hearing a child's cries, the goats' bleating, coming from my grandfather's basement, and the ultimate proof was bloody matter found in Mendel's garbage. The bloody matter was red goat droppings, the result of my mother's scoring a couple bags of beets gone bad. The police arrested Mendel, and a lynch mob was ready to tear him apart. He survived, and the police released him when the boy reappeared the next market day. Nobody apologized, because even if he was innocent this time, he must have committed a ritual murder some other time. After all, that is what "Christ killers" did.

My mother hated this period of her life; I am convinced her focus on appearances and drive to make money stemmed from those days. She resented being looked down upon by the more affluent members of the Jewish community who treated her with contempt, and to the bitter end, she never forgave her well-to-do half brothers and sisters for refusing to help.

She had no time for a leisurely, idyllic childhood. She had to grow up fast, and ever the enterprising spirit, started doing odd jobs around town when she was seven. She tutored other kids, ran errands, helped in local stores, and by the time she was eight, she had earned enough money to buy her own bed. For years she'd shared hers with two sisters, and her own bed was the modern equivalent of getting one's own room. She loved school, dreamt of going to the university and becoming a lawyer, but her parents, especially Mendel, imbued with the values of their class and generation, wouldn't think of it. Education beyond elementary school was dangerous, a waste of time for girls. It might distract them from the important things a woman needed to know, keeping house, cooking, taking care of children. The Rothschilds educated their daughters, but they were rich. Their daughters didn't need to know how to cook and clean, they could afford servants. Educating girls was unwise. One heard rumors about university educated women. Nobody in Pultusk had met one, but people said they dressed like wanton women, smoked cigarettes, read gentile books, and some, God forbid, even married goyim. No, thank you! After the fourth grade, her parents apprenticed my mother to a shopkeeper where she worked until the age of twenty, when my father appeared next door.

While neither would ever admit to finding the other the least bit attractive, my parents agreed to marry under considerable pressure from all sides. Both recognized they were an embarrassment to their families and couldn't afford to be choosy. In the matrimonial market, they were equivalent to three-day-old bread, well past their prime. My mother, while pretty, carried the baggage of having no dowry. She was an unmarriageable twenty-year-old "spinster." She had to grab this opportunity or emigrate to America like her two half-sisters Emma and Heivet, who hoped that in the New World even a girl without a dowry could find a husband.

They married and lived unhappily ever after. A year after the wedding, my mother gave birth to a baby girl named Hannah. Hannah caught a cold and died a week later. My mom had a nervous breakdown and went into a deep fit of depression. The local doctor didn't know how to help her but thought having another child might make her forget the loss. And so, a year later I arrived on the scene, all 14 pounds of me. The next three years were uneventful. Buoyed by my mother's energy, the business flourished. My parents became well-established members of the thriving Jewish community and gained a wide circle of friends. I remember gatherings in our living room filled with lively and loud conversation over endless glasses of tea.

My existence was idyllic. I would rummage through the marvels in the shop or play in the yard with my best friend, our next-door neighbor's daughter, Celinka. With her blue eyes, rosy cheeks, and long blond Shirley Temple curls, she looked like an archetypal Polish doll, despite being Jewish. We were inseparable and spent endless hours together. Our parents were busy. Her father was the town's pharmacist, and as long as no one got hurt, they left us alone. I never saw Celinka after we moved into the ghetto. We settled at opposite ends of the enclave. I didn't think of her for many years until I saw the little girl with the red coat in *Schindler's List*. That scene snuck up on me, broke down my defenses, and just for a moment, I couldn't repress and intellectualize the memories and knowledge of what happened to so many people I loved. I cried for my first best friend, so pretty, so full of life and laughter, such a shameless tease and flirt even at three. She never had time to grow up, become a woman, and experience life because she died at five in a gas chamber in Treblinka.

I stopped myself after a while and regained control. I wish I could say that I repressed the memories just to avoid the pain of knowing what happened to Celinka, grandma Rachel, grandpa Mendel and so many others, but if truth be told I don't want to relive the fear, I don't want to experience again the panic, the constant dread one mistake, one false step, one unguarded word, one unexpected stroke of bad luck would land us in front of a firing squad or in a cattle car on a train headed for Treblinka.

When I was about two-and-a-half grandma Rachel came to stay with us. She was almost ninety years old but as vigorous as a woman thirty years younger. Voluminous petticoats and a floor length dark dress covered her squat, sturdy body. I remember her broad, red, wrinkled, always smiling face topped by the traditional sheitel, a wig, with a bun in back. She looked like a big, warm, comforting tea-cozy, and I was crazy about her. Grandma Rachel took over running the house while my mom concentrated on running the store. She refused to answer questions about her age and became very brusque with anyone who inquired about it. However, when it was convenient, she used it to her advantage. She sipped vodka throughout the day but was quick to point out it was only for medicinal reasons, "The heart is like a pump," she would say, "when you get to my age it has a tendency to stop, and you need a drop of schnapps to give it a jolt and get it started again." She also developed uncontrollable eye twitches, which could only be cured by whatever delicacy she craved at the moment. My parents, usually my mom, had to run around town to get the creamed herring, marzipan, or whatever was the medicinal food du jour.

Grandma Rachel felt the need to justify her nipping because Jews judged drinking on other than festive occasions (and even then, only in paltry amounts) to be common; something "they" did. Abstinence differentiated us from "them," and proved that though they might beat and oppress us, we were more refined and morally superior. An ugly scene I observed at an early age during a visit to Grandma Rachel's farm reinforced for me the lesson that drinking results in brutal and unseemly behavior.

I must have been about two years old, but the experience was so scary it became embedded forever in my memory. Across the road from Grandma Rachel's farm was a kretchma (a bar) where the local farmers came to drink, especially on market day when they had money. I was sitting on a wagon in front of the farmhouse watching the bar when two peasants emerged from the kretchma and started fighting with knives. To a scared two-year-old, the knives seemed enormous, as big as sabers. I sat there, too afraid to move, and watched the blood flow. The violence horrified me, but I couldn't take my eyes off the fight. The two combatants were too drunk to do significant damage, other than a few cuts here and there. After a while, I saw them stop and stumble over to the well where they washed off the blood and tottered back into the tavern. When I told Grandma Rachel and my aunts Blimtcha and Laitcha, who lived with her, about the fight, they used the opportunity to drive home the point about the stupidity of drinking and how it made goyim behave like animals.

During this same visit, I experienced one of the many acts of loving-kindness that were so typical of Grandma Rachel. According to my mom, I was toilet trained by the age of one, but my self-control at night was still tenuous. One morning I woke up in a wet bed. Afraid my grandma would find out I'd wet my bed, I planned to escape detection of my "shame" by refusing to get up. Ever the optimist, I hoped to stay in bed long enough for the sheets to dry. Grandma Rachel, mother to 11 children and 70 grandchildren, had no trouble diagnosing my dilemma. She offered me an easier and far more graceful way out. "Did the white hen wet your bed, by any chance? We are having the worst time with her. Try as we might, we can't train her to make in the barnyard. She keeps sneaking in at night into our beds and wets them. What shall we do with her? Maybe we should give her a taste of her own medicine?" With these words, she walked me out into the yard where she held the white chicken and told me to pee on the offending fowl.

Toddlers are notorious for low scores on the moral character scale, so I didn't confess and save the innocent bird. I remember performing the act and strutting away with my chest puffed out and an, "I hope this will teach you," thrown over my shoulder at the wet and bemused chicken. I don't know how grandma and my aunts stopped themselves from bursting out laughing, but somehow, they did as they led me to a triumphant breakfast. Years later, when I realized how thoughtful and ingenious they had been in protecting the dignity of a little boy, my heart filled with gratitude and love.

I loved Grandma Rachel; she was the one adult who always had time for me. I would follow her around as she did her chores during the day, and we often slept together in the same bed at night. Hardened by years of hard work on the farm, she had the strength and nimbleness of a woman half her age. She didn't need to go to the gym to stay in shape; she just kept working. An example of her physical ability I viewed as a fun thing to watch then but fills me with awe now when I feel the aches and pains of "old age" at 80, was the fattening of the Passover turkey. My parents bought a turkey for the Seder a few weeks before the holiday. To ensure it would be a proper centerpiece for the meal, Grandma Rachel undertook fattening the unfortunate bird. Twice a day, she'd roll pieces of bread into long cylinders she stored in her apron pockets. She chased down the terrified Tom, got behind him, hiked up her voluminous skirts, and gripped him between her legs. Once she immobilized the struggling bird, she forced open its beak and shoved the bread down its throat. Few people, of any age, can perform this task, something I am sure the turkey population appreciates.

In September 1939, when I was three, war broke out. The Germans had no trouble defeating the Polish army which, although brave, was ill-equipped for twentieth-century warfare. German tanks decimated Polish cavalry regiments who charged them. The German army occupied all of Poland in three weeks and soon after notified our town's Jews, we had to move to a ghetto on the edge of town. Faced with the thought of going to a ghetto, Grandma Rachel returned home to Prostyn to stay with Laitcha, Blimtcha and Laitcha's two small children. This was the last time I saw her. I was heartbroken to lose my favorite person, but you have little control over other people's actions when you are three. I was told Grandma Rachel and my aunts were part of the first group killed in Treblinka, the death camp the Nazis built on land once owned by Grandpa Moishe.

PART TWO

The War Years

3

The Ghetto

I was three years old when we moved into the Wolomin Ghetto in the late fall of 1939. It was a sizeable area of gracious, but uninsulated, summer cottages. Six-foot high barbed wire enclosed the Ghetto. Railroad tracks ran along one side, and perpendicular to the tracks were a smallish lake and a swimming beach. The other two sides adjoined wheat fields and grazing meadows. My family shared a three-bedroom house with two other families.

My maternal grandfather, Mendel Brzoza, joined us a few months after we moved there. He was on the way to see my parents when German soldiers captured him. They tied him to a tree, beat him with the butts of their guns, ripped out pieces of his beard by hand, and left him to die in subzero weather. He remained tied to the tree for three days until farmers found him half dead and brought him to our house. He was 86 years old, a tall man with the traditional long gray beard who, my Mom told me, was as vigorous as a man half his age until his mistreatment by the Germans. Though he survived this horrible ordeal, he was never the same again. The exposure to extreme cold and the beating left him paralyzed from the waist down. We heard after the war that his wife Rana, and my mom's youngest sister Zisa, tried to run away to Russia, but Ukrainians massacred them by beheading, along with many other Jews.

There was an interesting reversal of fortune in the social structure of our community. The shoemakers, tailors, and other craft workers who had been at the bottom of the social ladder were still busy performing their functions and earning a living. After all, bread still had to be baked, shoes needed mending and people needed clothes, but the pre-ghetto shop-keeping aristocracy was out of business. They had nothing to sell, there was no supply of any goods other than necessities, and even smugglers concentrated only on food. Ex-store owners like my dad wandered around with nothing to do, living off their savings.

The community tried to maintain a sense of order and normalcy in the ghetto by recreating the traditional institutions such as schools, synagogues, a mikvah (ritual bath) and even a small theater group. Every Friday afternoon, just as before the war, each family brought their covered pot of cholent, a thick stew of potatoes, beans, and meat bones to the baker. He would put it in the oven overnight so that no one would violate the Sabbath by cooking. We would pick it up the next day on the way home from the synagogue. This was the traditional Saturday afternoon meal. I still remember the comforting heartburn that followed its consumption and helped one remain awake after this heavy repast.

We heard, but couldn't believe, horrible tales about death camps; the stories became all too real when we saw the long cattle car trains packed with people from the Warsaw ghetto on their way to Treblinka. Sometimes, when the trains stopped for a few minutes alongside our barbed wire fence, we saw hands emerge through openings and heard anguished voices begging for water. Of all the things I grew to fear, winding up in one of these cars became the scariest. I stopped going to see Holocaust-related movies after seeing *The Pawnbroker*. Rod

Steiger played a survivor who had flashbacks of his child slipping out of his arms, crushed to death in one of those cars by the close-packed hysterical crowd of human sardines. I left the theater and sat in my car, unable to drive, shaking and speechless for a long while. The cattle-car scene reminded me the war years weren't just a dreadful dream; they happened! I felt the pawnbroker's unbearable pain in my deepest core. My God! Can you imagine the horror? To feel your child, slip out of your grasp, struggle against the immovable mass of humanity, and hear him die as he cries out to you for help. Sitting there, I knew empathy hadn't caused my paralysis. It was uncontrollable fear. It wasn't 1964. I wasn't safe in a theater in Philadelphia. It was 1941, and I was on that train going to Treblinka. I hadn't escaped.

Considering the times, we spent two uneventful, calm years in the ghetto, spiced only by my mother's resourceful handling of regular confrontations with death. The Germans allowed the purchase of a controlled amount of food, but it wasn't enough to feed the ghetto population. Freelance entrepreneurs like my mom supplied the rest. They smuggled in supplies purchased from Polish farmers. This was a dangerous activity, and my mom was the only woman involved, as far as I know. German gendarmes shot on the spot any Jew caught outside of the ghetto and few smugglers survived for any length of time, but hunger provided a steady supply of replacements.

My mom, who never lacked daring or confidence in her abilities at any age, was in her mid-twenties and at the peak of her physical and intellectual powers. She couldn't just sit around, spend her days gossiping. Knowing her, I am sure smuggling was more than just an opportunity to make a buck. It was a challenge and an opportunity to prove her competence. Her unshakeable confidence in her own invincibility, an uncanny ability to analyze situations and improvise unfettered by any small-minded requirements to stick to the truth, allowed her to escape death time and time again.

Two stories among many will give you a flavor of her modus operandi. The Germans always set up ambushes for smugglers. One day, we saw two gendarmes along with two Polish boys hide behind bushes near the spot my mother used to sneak in and out of the ghetto. The boys knew the local Jews and identified them to the soldiers who couldn't differentiate between Jews and Gentiles. We could see them from inside the barbed wire, but they were invisible to my mom as she approached the fence.

A crowd of potential "mourners" gathered near our house, the air filled with excited anticipation like that at a bullfight or a NASCAR race where the spectators hope to see the bullfighter gored, or a spectacular car crash. My dad paced back and forth, his face tight, his hands buried in his pockets while women in the crowd who bemoaned my fate as a certain future orphan hugged me. I was too young to grasp what was happening, but I cried because I couldn't breathe with my face mashed against the ample bellies of the eager comforters, and my mom wasn't there to rescue me.

In the late afternoon, my mother emerged from the woods walking her bicycle with a 200-pound bag of wheat slung over its frame. She was halfway across the meadow between the woods and the fence when the German soldiers and their youthful accomplices jumped out from behind the bushes. When she saw them, she didn't panic and try to run away like your standard issue human being. As calmly as possible, under the circumstances, she assessed the situation and decided she had an edge. She spoke both Polish and German, while her opponents knew only their own tongue.

The boys needed to know only one German word, JUDE (Jew), to accomplish their dirty work, so she beseeched them not to give her away. "We must tell them who you are, or they will beat us," they whined. With a look of utter disbelief and a voice filled with outraged Germanic indignation, my mother demanded to know why these brave soldiers allowed Polish scum to refer to them as filthy swine. Taken in by her obvious sincerity, and inspired by her righteous outrage, the gendarmes turned on the boys who ran away to avoid a beating.

With the field cleared, my mother coolly asked the gendarmes for directions to a nearby village. She was visiting her aunt's farm and was carrying a bag of pig feed. Unfamiliar with the area, she'd lost her way and was ever so grateful to run into these two gallant gentlemen. Informed she had almost stumbled into the ghetto, she crossed herself, "Jesus, Maria!" spat on the ground to show her disapproval of the cursed race, and armed with excellent directions from her newfound friends, went back to the woods. She waited until she was sure the soldiers left and marched her bicycle with the bag of wheat into the ghetto.

Anyone else would have called it quits after such a close call, but not her; she was back out there the very next day. German soldiers caught her many times, but she always talked herself out of trouble with some variation of the visiting relative who'd lost her way. She would come home, her cheeks red with excitement, eager to share with anyone who would listen how once again she had outsmarted the enemy.

She ran out of luck when the chief of police, a local *Volksdeutsch*, a Pole whose family had German origins, caught her. He recognized her and was taking her to the German headquarters, where she knew the Germans would shoot her. He refused all pleas for mercy, and for once, she thought her luck had run out. With nothing to lose, she played her last desperate card. She remembered her captor, a domineering bully with everyone else, feared his wife. Somehow, she had to use this bit of local gossip to affect her usual Houdini performance. She assumed a resigned countenance, assured him she understood he couldn't let her go, accepted her fate, but as a mother about to die asked for only one last favor. She wanted to bid goodbye to her only child, and since she couldn't do it in person, she wanted another mother, one who could understand how she felt, to transmit her last words to her poor orphaned baby. Could he, on the way to the police station, stop at his house and let her tell his wife what she wanted her to say to me? Her plea moved this German lackey, and he agreed to stop at home.

When his wife, who my mom knew also had a four-year-old boy, heard her sad request, she burst into tears and lit into her husband. What kind of animal did she marry? Picking on poor defenseless women! Maybe someday he would take her and their poor child to the firing squad. She didn't want to hear anything about his duty to the state, chased him out of the house, and when she was sure he'd left, sent my mother home with an orange for me. In Poland, especially during the war, an orange was as rare as a unicorn. When my mother returned to the ghetto, everyone gathered to view this wonderful golden fruit. They passed it from hand to hand, examined it, smelled it, and placed it in the center of the table for general admiration. After a few days, my parents peeled the orange and gave me one segment a day. I took my time and consumed it with the respect such an exotic marvel deserved.

Everyone knew it was only a question of time until the Germans liquidated our ghetto. It was a holding pen and when they were ready, they would pack us into the trains, and we would join Warsaw's Jews in the gas chambers of Treblinka. My mom started preparing for this eventuality early on. She bought false identity papers naming her Karolina Wojcicki. My father was Jan Kasprzak, and I was his son Mieczyslaw Kasprzak. They started calling me Mietek for short, and no matter how many times my name changed as we went from country to country in later years, to my parents, I remained Mietek.

During her smuggling forays, she inquired if any of the farmers might hide us and at what price. She had to find the right person. Some farmers, enticed by the opportunity to make money, might risk their lives and hide us, but would they be willing to last the course, or would they panic along the way and throw us out into the cold? Even worse, once we were in their home, would they kill us and take our money since we had no law to protect us? It took her a while, but after much soul- searching, she picked a farmer named Pashnick, and when she found out from a paid informant on the police force the Germans planned to liquidate the ghetto the next day, she moved us to his root cellar where we remained for three years.

I remember my dad waking me up in the middle of the night; he told me we had to get dressed and leave the ghetto. Like a typical five-year-old, I was excited. It sounded fun, an adventure. I followed my parents and obeyed their order to be silent as we squeezed through the barbed wire and marched in darkness through fields to our destination.

Reflecting on that night from an adult perspective, I often wondered what thoughts crossed my parents' minds that day and night. What internal moral debates did they go through? They had information about the fate of the ghetto's inhabitants but didn't share it with anyone, even their closest friends, dooming them to a certain death. I assume they feared the news would spread and the resulting panic and attempts at mass escape would alert the Germans, endangering their own chances. Even harder for my mom had to be leaving behind her paralyzed father, who couldn't walk, and her brother Moishe and his family. Moishe had no money and lived off charity in the ghetto. Figuring she didn't have enough capital to support both families, my mother opted to maximize our own survival chances.

It's easy, sitting in a comfortable chair in a safe environment, to wax philosophical and quarrel with their decisions, but these were not safe and normal times, and the people who lived to tell the tale were those who focused on only one goal, surviving for at least one more day. We heard after the war that the Germans packed Moishe and his family with the rest of the ghetto population on cattle cars to Treblinka, where the Nazis exterminated them as if they were vermin, not innocent human beings. We heard after liberation from a Polish policeman who was there that Grandpa Mendel's death was swifter, but not kinder. Since he couldn't move himself, soldiers dragged him by the heels down a flight of stairs from his bedroom, his head hitting each step on the way down. They put him out of his misery when they shot him at the bottom of the stairs.

4

The Cellar

We arrived at the Pashnicks' just before dawn and were "welcomed" by our hosts to what we would call home for the next three years. The house was an ideal hiding place. It was far removed from other farmhouses, and the Pashnicks didn't socialize. The downstairs, the only part of the house I ever saw, comprised a large kitchen with the traditional wood or coal cooking stove, and an adjoining sizeable room that served as both a dining and living room. During frigid winter nights, it also served as a dormitory where we all slept on the floor, huddled around the potbellied stove that provided the only heat in the house. Behind the house was an extensive field where the Pashnicks grew potatoes, turnips, cabbages, and other assorted vegetables. To the right were sheds with farm tools and stacks of drying bricks of turf (peat) for cooking and heating the house.

Our residence was the root cellar where the Pashnicks stored their crops of potatoes, turnips, rutabagas, and broken furniture. It was a sizeable space, seven or eight feet high, lit during the day by two small ground level windows, but pitch dark at night. The cellar floor was hard packed dirt, and we sat and slept on burlap bags filled with straw. The air was still and redolent with the sweetish smell of rotting potatoes.

You accessed the cellar from the kitchen through a trapdoor that opened onto a flight of wooden stairs. It was fine for hiding from casual visitors, but a death trap in case of a search by the Germans or the police. My dad devised and built a very ingenious hiding place for such an eventuality. The cellar trap door was about six feet from the kitchen's wall, and long wide wooden planks placed one next to the other were the floor. He used a hacksaw to cut the nails that held the planks between the trapdoor and the wall, left the nail heads in the wood, and dug a hole underneath. You could get in the hole by lifting the planks, and when they were back in place, the floor looked normal. The hole was about five by five-by-five feet, just enough space for my parents to sit on the ground with their knees up, and me on my mother's lap.

We used the hole only once when gendarmes did a random search of farmhouses looking for God knows what. I remember sitting there, trembling, comforted by the warmth of my mother's body and the feel of her arms around me. The search seemed interminable. I had irrepressible urges to scratch myself, to clear my throat, to move, but knew that any slight noise or movement might give us away. I forced myself to stay still and escaped in my mind far away to a desert where, hidden behind dunes and armed to the teeth, my trusty companions and I waited in ambush for a column of German soldiers. We killed them all!

After the war, we found out my father's cousins Mania and Leon Fryd had gone through a similar experience, but with a far more tragic outcome. Mania was pregnant when they went into hiding and soon thereafter gave birth to a little girl. I am not sure of the exact nature of their hideout, but during a search by gendarmes, the baby cried out. Leon, one of the gentlest and kindest men I've ever known, tried to stifle her cries by putting his hand over the baby's mouth. The Germans didn't find them, but when Leon took his hand off the baby's mouth, she was dead. Leon never recovered. He'd be fine for a while, but then lapse into periods of deep depression that made him unable to function and enjoy his wife or his surviving two children.

The Pashnicks were in their forties and had two young adult children, a son in his early twenties, and an eighteen or nineteen-year-old daughter. Mr. Pashnick was large and burly, with a pleasant face dominated by an enormous walrus mustache. He was a simple man who just wanted to do his job as train conductor, grow his vegetables, and have time to enjoy a few ounces of vodka in peace.

Peace, however, was a scarcity in the Pashnick household ruled with an iron fist by Mrs. Pashnick, an unhappy and disappointed woman. I don't know what dreams she'd nurtured as a young girl, but they were far different from her present life. Filled with rage at the reality of her existence, she exuded anger and unhappiness from every pore in her small, hard, unyielding body. She dressed in drab-colored rayon housecoats buttoned in front. Two angry black eyes glared out of her hard face. She plaited her black hair sprinkled with silver into a long braid wound into a Danish on top of her head. She clumped around the house, clothed in an aura of intense resentment, cursing her fate and the bastards who'd contributed to it.

We could hear her from the cellar, through the cracks in the kitchen floorboards, venting her spleen as she went about cooking or cleaning, "Smigly-Rydz (the Polish prime and defense minister before the war) you son of a bitch! Don't worry, you said. We will teach the Germans a lesson they'll never forget; they'll never mess with us again. Yeah, you motherfucker! You're hiding in London with that other cocksucker Moscicki (the Polish president), living high on the hog, eating fancy cakes made with fine flour, while I can only get this crap. You try making kluskis (noodles) with this garbage! I fuck both your mothers, bastard whores!"

We became used to her rants; they became background noise. But we were always careful to stay on her good side since whether we could stay or had to go was solely in her hands. Her only soft spot was her darling son, Tadek, but even he dashed her fondest hopes. Like many doting mothers, she mistook his languor and general ineffectiveness for an intellectual bent. Her world collapsed when he flunked out of the university and had to take a job as a train conductor with his father. This was just one more unfair turn of fortune dumped on her by unkind fates and stoked the fires of her bitter resentment.

Her daughter, Ciesia, inherited her father's good nature. She worked in a shop in town and spent much of her time daydreaming about a gimpy-legged young man, Yurek, whom she desperately wanted to marry or at least date. However, he didn't seem to return her obvious interest. Since her mother was disinterested in discussing her romantic problems, she often came to my mom for help in deciphering Yurek's actions and plotting how to get him to realize she was the only woman for him.

As time passed, we developed a routine. The day revolved around the three meals: bread, potatoes, turnips, rutabagas, and an occasional piece of fatback. This Spartan diet left me with a lifelong hatred for turnips, and I am not too crazy about rutabagas either, but bread and potatoes to this day are my ultimate comfort foods. The bread was dense, dark and filling. I dread to think what would have happened if we'd had to subsist on Wonder bread. Sometimes we would get a few garlic cloves and would rub the bread's crust with them. The smell of garlic permeated its coarse texture and changed it from just hunger-quenching to a gastronomic treat. My mouth still waters when I think about it. No high-priced dish prepared at a five-star restaurant can compete with the pleasure we derived from this gustatory experience. The Pashnicks grew their own potatoes and turnips, but feared an unusual increase in bread purchases might arouse suspicion in town, so Mr. Pashnick bought extra bread in Warsaw, and carried it home from the train station.

To help me deal with the boredom of endless hours with nothing to do, my father told me tales about life in Polish forests. I especially liked the drama of stories about farmers chased by bands of wolves. What a relief when they escaped to safety in the nick of time. He also carved chess pieces out of wood and taught me how to play. Both parents taught me how to read and some rudiments of arithmetic, but I escaped my dreary surroundings through a form of mental television: daydreaming. I created my own programming, action adventures in exotic locales. Indiana Jones had nothing on me. I, too, always emerged victorious after escaping from the clutches of colorful villains, and the best part was, I could be fearless. As the writer, director, and producer of my personal dramas, I had total control. Nothing bad could ever happen to me in my stories. I might have no control over the stifling, boring and dangerous reality I lived, but I sure as hell could make my fantasy world exciting and safe.

As a five-year-old who'd never been away from his small town, and even smaller ghetto, I had little experience as material for my stories other than what I heard from my parents, and what I could glean from the meager reading collection available in the Pashnick household. This comprised Henryk Sienkiewicz's "Quo Vadis" and his multi-volume historical epic "With Sword and Fire," a gory tale of the struggle between Poles and invading Tartars filled with bloody tales of killing and torture. It gave me nightmares, but I kept rereading it because it was better than nothing. The only other reading material was the Pashnicks' collection of Sunday school pamphlets put out by the church for the moral edification of Polish children.

Reading these hateful tracts, it was easy to identify one source of the rabid anti-Semitism so prevalent in Poland. I will uplift you with two of these 'moral' lessons that best exemplify a couple of favorite themes. The first one covers Jews as dishonest Shylocks you must avoid at all costs. In this tale, little Stanislaw was looking with lust at the ice cream vendor's cart, dreaming of eating one of his delicious, sweet cones. Unfortunately, he didn't have the money to buy one, and he didn't want to ask his mother because he knew the family had little to spend on luxuries. Just then, his mother asked him to go buy tea, and this gave the Devil an opportunity to tempt poor little Stanislaw into committing a sin. Stanislaw knew his mother always bought her groceries from the Polish merchant several blocks away and never from the Jew next door, even though the Jew charged less.

"Stanislaw, why don't you buy the tea from the Jew and use the zloty you save to buy yourself this yummy ice cream," the Devil whispered in the innocent boy's ear.

"But isn't it wrong to buy from Jews?" asked Stanislaw.

"Of course, it's wrong, but we'll keep it our secret. You can buy the tea from the Jew and eat the ice cream during the time your mom thinks you are walking all those blocks to and from the Polish store, and no one will be the wiser for it."

Stanislaw knew it was wrong, but the lure of the ice cream was too strong, and he gave in to the devil's urgings. He was just swallowing the last bit of the cone as he came into his house, bearing the tea he bought from the Jew.

"Ah! There you are," said his mother. "You've been such a good boy getting me the tea without complaining. Here, take this zloty and buy yourself an ice cream cone." Little Stanislaw's face reddened with shame as he shambled out the door. He now realized how wrong he had been, and he promised himself never again to listen to the Devil and buy from Jews.

In the second story, Jacob is a usual dirty and depraved Jewish kid in elementary school. One day, the teacher shows the school children a new school flag they will carry in a procession during the holiday season. Jacob, who is used to living in filthy surroundings, is all-agog. He has seen nothing so shiny, so clean, and so beautiful. It is so different from his dirty home crawling with vermin. That afternoon a fire breaks out in the school and all the panicked students run out screaming with fear. Only Jacob remains behind. There is so little of any esthetic value in his miserable life. The flag is his first exposure to beauty, and he can't stand the thought of it being destroyed. Blinded and choked by smoke and burnt by flames, he stumbles out, clutching the flag to his grimy little chest. Jacob spends several weeks recovering from his injuries, but when he returns, the teacher chooses him to carry the flag in the holiday parade. You never saw a prouder little Jew strutting in front of the crowd, gripping the pole of the beautiful flag in his filthy little hands with a big smile on his dirty face. This just proves that the lowest of the low, even dirty Jews (I grew up believing "dirty Jew" was just one word), can be affected by beauty.

Each month, my parents paid the Pashnicks a fixed sum of money for hiding us in their cellar. I am not sure of the amount, but it was worth whatever we paid them. They risked their lives and those of their children. We heard stories of Jewish families caught on other farms and German soldiers executing not only the Jews, but also the Polish family that kept them. We all lived in constant fear, and when Mrs. Pashnick heard a rumor that German soldiers were planning a random search of farms, she told us to leave the farm for the day and go somewhere else. She didn't care where. We left before dawn and went to the local cemetery. It was a logical place to hide for the day; it was a couple of miles away from the village, surrounded by walls and wheat fields, and unlikely to have many visitors. If anyone questioned why we were there, we could pretend we were visiting the grave of a dead relative. I never went outside during the day for two years, and while conscious of the danger we were in, I was ecstatic.

It was a beautiful, bright May morning, so different from the permanent semi-darkness I'd become accustomed to. The air, unlike the musty cellar, smelled sweet with the aroma of field flowers. Best of all, narrow walls and mounds of root vegetables did not restrict me. I could run forever through what seemed an endless expanse of the cemetery. It was a banner day, and while I realized the necessity, I was reluctant to return to the farmhouse after nightfall.

My parents never fully trusted the Pashnicks, afraid they might kill us or at least rob us if they thought we had the money with us. They told them we had it buried somewhere and every month my mom went out at night, wandered around for a few hours and gave them the money when she returned. This may sound paranoid, but remember, only the paranoid survived. The danger was real; we had no law to protect us. Anyone could assault us and do with us whatever they wanted. What could we do? Complain to the police? A bunch of teenagers almost raped my mother on one of her nocturnal sorties. She escaped, her clothes torn but unscathed, only because of a fortunate intervention by one of her old customers who was walking his dog and chased the horny hoodlums away.

We did not know how long the war would drag on and my parents worried their limited amount of money might run out, so my mother came up with another one of her patented cunning schemes. One night she went to see the Zarembas, a well-off family in town, and offered them a deal she hoped they couldn't refuse.

"You know how rich Jews are," she told Mrs. Zaremba, "and we were the wealthiest Jews in town. However, we made a terrible mistake. We didn't remain liquid. We never trusted banks, so we put all our money, a fortune, into gold and jewels, millions and millions of zloty in diamonds, rubies, emeralds, and pearls. You should see how beautiful they are, how they sparkle. We were stupid, we never thought about needing money for an emergency, so we buried them in our backyard before going to the ghetto, and now we have a terrible problem. We are richer than Croesus but have no cash, and unless we get some help, we won't survive, and all those millions will rot in the ground."

Once she baited the hook, my mom reeled it in. She picked Mrs. Zaremba as her victim because she knew her to be both vain and greedy. The thought of all those jewels decorating her fingers, wrists, and neck was a more powerful attraction than just money. With my mother's help, she came up with a solution to our problem. The Zarembas would give us enough money each month to pay the Pashnicks, and in return, when the war was over, we would give them half our fortune.

My mother "reluctantly" agreed to the deal after arguing for a less generous split. She pointed out the Zarembas would put out only a measly few thousand zlotys in return for a share of a fortune worth hundreds of millions. Even ten percent would make them rich. When the Zarembas wouldn't budge, she gave in, and with a deep sigh, conceded she had to be a realist. They had the upper hand, and she had to accept the exorbitant fifty/fifty split. Our fifty percent would still leave us millions. For the Zarembas, my mother's haggling was proof the fictitious buried treasure was real and secured their stake in the partnership.

Any rational person, not driven by greed and the myth of ill-gotten Jewish wealth, would see that a small bicycle shop couldn't generate that kind of wealth even in a thousand successful years, but my mother worked hard to keep the fantasy alive and growing during each monthly visit. She described, in glowing detail, the various pieces of jewelry and discussed which ones would look best on Mrs. Zaremba. She advised them on the house they'd build with the money, and how best to furnish it. She helped them plan trips, in exquisite detail, to Paris and the Riviera, and they spent many evenings discussing the wonderful life we'd all live after the war. She became Zarembowa's best friend, who eagerly awaited her monthly visits. During one of these visits, Zarembowa confided to my mom how she kept her shape despite a ravenous appetite; she ate all she wanted, then forced herself to vomit.

We'd never heard of bulimia and thought the behavior bizarre, but it also filled us with the fury French peasants felt upon hearing Marie Antoinette's suggestion they should eat cake if they had no bread. Here we were starving, subsisting on bread, potatoes and turnips and the Queen Bee, of her own volition, threw up food we could only dream of. Whatever qualms, and I don't believe for a minute she had any, my mother might have had about exploiting the Zarembas' greed and gullibility; this disclosure quashed them.

The Zaremba connection was a lifesaver. Not only did it provide us with financial security, but towards the war's end, it led us to our last hiding place when we had to leave the Pashnicks. For me, the Zaremba connection provided an unexpected but wonderful bonus. My mother brought me a book each time she visited the Zarembas. I rationed my reading. The book had to last a month, and I allowed myself only so many pages a day. The stories filled me with wonder, broke down the cellar's walls, allowed me to roam unfettered through exciting new worlds, where I could imagine further adventures beyond those described by the author.

Evenings were the best part of the day; once it turned dark, we could come up from the cellar and sit in the kitchen with the Pashnicks. During spring and summer, when the windows were open, we could smell the sweet fragrance of lilac bushes and acacia trees; it was intoxicating. Sometimes we even went outside to help dig up potatoes. The farm was so isolated there was little chance of being spotted in the evening twilight. It was a treat to be out in the fresh air, with no walls confining our movements, feeling the breeze moving over our faces and bodies instead of the unvarying stillness and stuffiness of the cellar. During the winter, it was too cold to sleep in the cellar and we slept on the kitchen floor around the potbellied stove. We washed, as well as we could, in a sink filled with hot water my mother boiled every Saturday night. She tried to get the lice out of our hair with a very fine toothcomb, but we could never get rid of them no matter how hard we tried.

No matter how Jewish we were, Christmas became our favorite holiday. Christmas day we ate dinner with the Pashnicks around the dining room table, and what a glorious feast it was: fried pierogi filled with sauerkraut, a roasted goose, and chocolate cake. Even now, my mouth waters at the memory.

The war seemed to go on forever. Our only news came from the German-controlled radio in the kitchen, and gossip my mom heard from Mrs. Zaremba during her monthly visits. Mr. Pashnick was in Warsaw every day, but he was not interested in anything that didn't affect his daily life, so he wasn't a useful source.

We despaired when the German army marched inexorably east, but after a while, we sensed a turn in the tides of war and learned to read between the lines. German propaganda on the radio stopped reporting advances deep into the Russian homeland. The reports still trumpeted new German victories, but these "victories" were now brilliant tactical troop movements to superior strategic positions. Those new strategic positions were always west of the previous ones. Even without a map, we could visualize in our minds the steady retreat of the German army from Russia into Poland. For the first time, we could start dreaming about the possibility of freedom and not just rejoice we'd survived another day.

As thrilled as we were about the steady decline in the fortunes of the German army, the news that excited us most and filled us with pride, was the Warsaw ghetto uprising. Jews were taking up arms and fighting back. This was unheard of in our experience. We learned from an early age not to fight but run away when attacked by Gentiles, and if running was not an option, to absorb the blows and appeal to the attacker's pity and kindness. Like a defeated dog, we learned to expose our throat and beg for mercy.

While the radio reported no German casualties or any difficulties eliminating the "criminal Jewish bandits," we knew the Jews were holding their ground, and were the ones dishing out pain and death for a change. Every day for a month or more we heard about the end of the "cleanup" action, but the next day the cleanup was still in the last stages, as it was the next day and the day after. We were crushed when the inevitable occurred: the Germans prevailed and killed most of the fighters, except for a few who escaped through the sewers. We grieved for those who died, but also felt stronger. Those Jews proved we did not have to be the traditional ninety-pound weaklings; we had it in us to be Maccabees. The biblical stories of strong, heroic fighting Jews were not just a Bubbe Manseh (an old wives' tale). It was real.

As the relentless retreat west by the German army continued reducing its aura of invincibility, the Polish population became emboldened and less fearful of the Germans. Besides armed attacks and sabotage by the Polish underground, the Armja Krajowa (Homeland Army), the populace started taunting the occupying forces with insults and slogans painted on walls during the night. The Germans, like wounded bulls hounded by banderilleros, struck back with beatings, imprisonment and even executions, but the genie was out of the bottle. The inevitability of an eventual German defeat was clear and long pent-up rage oozed out of every crack in the Germans' tyrannical control. In early spring of 1944, the rebellion reached even our village. During the night, some "educated" young wit, conversant with German, painted the following couplet on the wall of the local army headquarters:

Hitler du dumme affe
Wo ist dein neue waffe.

This rhyme said, "Hitler, you dumb ape, where is your new weapon?" The new weapon they alluded to, was a centerpiece of much German propaganda during the latter part of the war. It would destroy the Allied armies and bring ultimate victory to the Third Reich.

Everyone thought it was just another colossal lie, generated by Goebel's fertile imagination, designed to bolster the morale of the retreating troops. Little did we know it was the atom bomb. I might not be sitting here if German scientists had produced one before the Americans.

The local commander was furious about such an affront to the Fuehrer. Unable to identify the author of the seditious couplet, he punished the entire town by rounding up dozens of young men and women and sending them off to forced, or if you prefer, slave labor in Germany. There was a general crackdown; even minor infractions ignored in the past were punished with beatings and/or imprisonment. The new harsh climate spooked the Pashnicks. They figured it was safer to quit while they were ahead and told us to leave. My parents tried to bluff them, refused to go, dared them to call the Germans who would shoot them along with us. The Paschnicks called their bluff, threatened to call in the local Polish underground, who would eliminate us without harming them. We knew they were right; the Armja Krajowa, like so many other Polish institutions, was anti-Semitic. We heard many stories about them killing Jews and were as afraid of them as of the Germans. We struck a compromise: they allowed my father and me to stay for forty-eight hours while my mother went looking for an alternative hiding place. When she didn't come back after two days, we had to leave with no place to go and no guarantee or even hope we would ever see her again.

5

Separation and Reunion

I missed my mom, but was excited to be free, unconfined by the cellar's four walls. Walking through wide-open fields, I fantasized about a new life full of freedom. We would hide in the woods, live a life full of adventure, and maybe even join a group of partisans and wage war on the Germans. This would be so much fun! The advantage of being eight years old is you don't have to think about boring practical aspects of life like food and shelter; I delegated these to my father while I concentrated on imagining our great new life.

I lived to tell this tale because my dad had a clearer idea of our needs. While I kept urging him to go straight to the forest, he followed a path towards a cluster of farmhouses where we ran into an old farmer, Mr. Oleksiak, who was hand tilling one of his fields. He recognized my dad, whom he knew from the prewar years. Oleksiak was tall and lean, his body hardened and stooped by years of manual labor. He wore dirty overalls, his stringy, grayish hair covered by a beat-up greasy cap. His face, like his frame, was lean, lined by deep furrows and dominated, like most Polish farmers his age, by a ragged walrus mustache that hung like bangs over his mouth. He was a widower in his sixties who lived alone in his large rambling farmhouse and cultivated his land by himself with occasional help from one of his sons. I don't know whether it was loneliness, kindheartedness or some other motive that made Oleksiak agree to let us stay with him; whatever it was, it saved our lives.

We stayed at Mr. Oleksiak's farm for two or three months, cloistered in a back bedroom. Time passed at a snail's pace. There were only the two of us. Mr. Oleksiak showed up only when it was time to bring us food, the ubiquitous bread, and potatoes. He was not much of a conversationalist. There were no books in his house, and we left the chess set at the Pashnicks, so we sat, day after day, buried in whatever thoughts allowed us to escape the cramped, dreary room.

We had one exciting, if you want to call it that, episode during our stay at Oleksiak's farm. One Sunday afternoon, the sudden arrival of two truckloads of German soldiers interrupted our usual routine of staring into space. They surrounded the farm and started rummaging through the buildings. We thought someone had snitched and told the gendarmes Oleksiak was harboring Jews. There was no way for us to escape; our room had only one door leading to the parlor and from there, the kitchen where we could hear the soldiers rummaging through cabinets. We sat petrified, holding our breaths, hoping for a miracle, but felt certain this was the end. With mounting panic, we heard the soldiers enter the parlor where Mr. Oleksiak was napping on the sofa, their boots' marching inexorably closer towards the closed bedroom door. Like an artistic directorial shot in a horror movie, we saw the doorknob turn in slow motion, then a guttural shout from outside and the doorknob turned back to its original position. The door stayed closed, and the boots ran out from the parlor. We heard more shouting in the yard, then after what seemed like an eternity, the soldiers got back on the trucks and rode away. Through it all we sat motionless, adrenaline racing through our bodies, trembling, unable to move, gasping for air, unsure of what happened and too numb to celebrate that once again we escaped certain death.

We found out later what happened from Mr. Oleksiak, who'd slept the sleep of the just or the old through the whole incident. The Germans weren't looking for Jews. Someone tipped them off Oleksiak's son was running an illegal still, and they came to confiscate it. The shout that saved us came from the barn, where a soldier found the son brewing his latest batch of vodka. Since they found what they were looking for, there was no point in searching the house further, and so, thanks to dumb luck, we got to live another day. Oleksiak's son, caught red-handed, admitted his guilt but swore to the Germans his father knew nothing about his illegal activities and so, lucky for us, they didn't arrest the old man. I don't know what happened to the son. It is likely the Germans sent him to a slave labor camp in Germany, and we left the farm soon after.

Spurred by our narrow escape, or maybe feeling lucky, my dad tried to find Mom. One night under the cover of darkness, he sought out our only contact, the Zarembas, and to his great joy, found out they knew where she was: fifty or sixty miles away on a farm owned by Mrs. Zaremba's aunt. When my mom left the Pashnicks, she went to the Zarembas to look for a fresh hiding place. They were her best hope, as long as they believed she was their key to untold hidden riches. They were unwilling to keep us themselves, but suggested an aunt who, along with her husband, was getting on in years and needed help to run their farm. My mom couldn't get back to us with the wonderful news, because for some unknown reason, the Germans imposed a temporary curfew, increased night patrols, and it wasn't safe to be out on the streets at night. When she returned to the Pashnicks, we were long gone, and her only choice was to go on to the aunt's house hoping that somehow, we would survive, and my father was smart enough to find her through the Zarembas.

During the two or three months my mother was on the farm, she made herself indispensable to the Ciepelowiczes, Mrs. Zaremba's aunt and uncle. My mother was in her late twenties, strong and full of energy. She made their life easy and though they were reluctant to take on the rest of us, they couldn't afford to lose her.

On the most wonderful day of my life, Mrs. Ciepelowicz showed up at Oleksiak's doorstep and took us to her farm by train. The train ride was dangerous; it was in daylight on a train full of people, with an occasional police officer or German soldier to help raise our blood pressure. My dad was blond and looked fine, especially with the walrus mustache he'd grown to appear more Polish, but he spoke Polish with a heavy Yiddish accent. Mrs. Ciepelowicz explained his silence, telling everyone he was an unfortunate cousin who was shell-shocked during the war. He was not only slow but lost his ability to speak. My Polish was fine, but with my jet-black curls, I looked the epitome of a Jewish kid. After three years in the cellar, I had a Casper the Friendly Ghost complexion. We hid my hair under a cap, and Mrs. Ciepelowicz, when asked about my deathly pallor, told the curious I had tuberculosis and she was taking me to the country, hoping fresh air would help my condition. These explanations created space around us. No one wanted to find out whether the "village idiot" was not only dumb but also violent, and people were as scared of tuberculosis as we are of the Coronavirus. The disease before the discovery of penicillin was fatal.

We got off the train late in the afternoon and walked several miles through woods. We reached the farmhouse at dusk and for me, our reunion was better than a hundred Christmases and birthdays combined. I had my mom back, and I couldn't stop crying. At last, I could let myself feel how much I had missed her. While separated, I didn't allow myself to think about her absence. I learned during our years in the cellar that it was useless to dwell on what I couldn't have, so I blocked out all thoughts of her. But here she was, alive and beautiful, and I clung to her, afraid she would disappear again.

I held on to her for a long time, but at my parents' insistence, I finally let go, and the perfect day continued. My mother served us bacon and eggs, fresh baked pumpernickel bread, and milk to wash it all down. This may seem a simple meal, but to me, it was a Lucullan feast; I hadn't seen, never mind eaten, eggs or milk for years, especially in the quantities dished out on my plate. No meal I've eaten since ever tasted as good.

After dinner, I lay down in my room on an actual bed with clean, ironed sheets. The window was wide open, and I could smell the wonderful scent of pine trees outside. To this day, when I smell the scent of pine trees, I'm filled with joy. It evokes memories of that wonderful night. I drifted into the most peaceful slumber. The sheets felt cool, my stomach was full of delicious food, my mom was next door, and all was well in the world.

6

Liberation

We spent the rest of the war on the farm, and for me those six months were idyllic. The farm had cows, goats, pigs, chickens, and an extensive vegetable garden. For the first time in years, we ate a rich diet of eggs, milk, meat and fresh vegetables besides the bread and potatoes we'd become used to. Best of all, I was free to roam in what seemed unlimited open space, unconfined by the four walls of a cellar or even a cramped room. The farm stood by itself, several miles from the village, nestled on the edge of a wooded plateau. We dared to live in the open, like normal farm folk trying to earn a living off the land. No one came to visit from the village, and the only people who knew of our existence on the farm, besides the Ciepelowiczes, were their tenants, a rather bizarre couple, a retired gimpy shoemaker, and his much younger wife.

The wife was a problem at first. She didn't buy Mrs. Ciepelowicz's story, doubted my mother was a young single mom widowed by the war, and my dad a shell-shocked idiot. She suspected we were Jewish and kept trying to get me to take off my pants. I always refused her requests, not because of any modesty. I was too innocent for that, but because I knew it was dangerous. The way Germans distinguished Jewish men from Poles was by checking for circumcised penises. In Poland, unlike the United States, circumcision was only a Jewish practice. When I told my mom about the tenant's wife's attempts to disrobe me, she put an end to this in her usual unique way. She often wondered why the couple who'd lived their entire lives in a big industrial city, Lodz, had retired to such an isolated spot in the country. Looking for an edge, she started spying on them. Some nights, she observed groups of men sneaking bundles into their place late at night, always leaving before dawn. She listened in at the window one night and learned the shoemaker was part of the communist underground, and a liaison for left-wing partisan groups.

Armed with this information, she approached him the next day and took him into her confidence. Told him she was a communist party member from a Warsaw cell and was hiding on the farm because the Gestapo had gotten onto her. She'd escaped in the nick of time before the Germans could arrest her. Thrilled to find a comrade, she was eager to join forces and fight the fascists, but worried his wife was causing trouble spreading stupid rumors she was Jewish. The last thing she needed was to attract attention to the farm through gossip. The gimp, happy to find an unexpected ally, promised to control his wife, which he did through a handful of well-reasoned and convincing blows. We heard her pleas for mercy and promises to keep her mouth shut from far off.

She never bothered me again and my mother added the job of helping the partisans to all her other chores. I still don't know how she found the time and energy to do it all. Not only did she clean the house, do the laundry, cook the meals, but she also fed the chickens and pigs, milked the cows and goats, and took care of the garden. Her boundless energy, which had no outlet while cooped up in the Pashnick's cellar, was let loose here. She thrived on the work. I don't remember her ever looking better or, considering the circumstances, happier. My dad spent most of the time sitting idle in the bedroom to maintain the image of the shell-shocked halfwit, but also because as a self-respecting ex-yeshiva student and Jewish small business owner, he had no experience or affinity for farm work.

While my mom kept the farm going, my dad sat thinking about God knows what. Each morning I drove a herd of goats to their pasture, with help from Ciapek, my faithful companion, and best friend, a lovable, floppy-eared, black-and-white dog of unknown and undistinguished ancestry. The goats, an unruly and perverse bunch, were hard to keep together both on the way to and from the pasture, but once we got there, they became absorbed in their favorite activity: eating. Ciapek and I could relax, except for the odd moment when a young buck would charge and butt me with his head. I loved these long, warm summer days sitting or lying in a meadow, breathing in fresh country air scented by the smell of crushed grass and rich earth, so different from the Pashnick's cramped cellar and the smell of rotting root vegetables.

I still spent most of my time daydreaming, but in these beautiful surroundings, the fantasies were gentler, and more hopeful. My favorite, which I kept refining and embellishing, was what would happen after the Germans were defeated. I didn't know how many Jews would still be alive when the war ended. For all I knew, all those I'd cared for were dead; we might be the only survivors.

In my fantasy, the few of us who survived became celebrities. After all, we were winners of an extended marathon of pain, fear, and deprivation, which only people like my mother, gifted with superhuman endurance and cunning, could hope to finish. There would be parades with us as the guests of honor and, after all the fawning and the hoopla were over, we would be whisked off on a plane to America where we'd be greeted by marching bands and live happily ever after. I settled on an airplane ride and America because I knew nothing about either and therefore could make both as fabulous as I wanted. When I was tired of daydreaming, I could watch the shapes of clouds lazily floating overhead, count the number of cars in a train passing on the railroad track in the distance, or run around with my buddy Ciapek.

By fall, we couldn't miss signs the war was coming to the hoped-for end. Not only did we hear about continual "strategic" retreats by the German army but we saw evidence of the rollback with our own eyes. From the plateau on which our farm was located, we saw the highway below choked with an endless line of horse-drawn wagons carrying the meager belongings and families of Ukrainians, Latvians, and Lithuanians, German allies fleeing the vengeful wrath of the pursuing Russian armies.

On some level, we empathized with these people who left their homes and possessions behind and fled for their lives; they didn't know what awaited them or even where they'd sleep that night. However, they were our enemies' allies who'd prospered while we suffered, and their plight, like snowdrops announcing the imminent arrival of spring, was a sign the Russian army and freedom were getting closer.

Tanks and truckloads of German soldiers soon followed the Ukrainians and Lithuanians. One of the retreating outfits chose our farmhouse as a temporary headquarters. We were all squeezed into one room while the officers took over the rest of the house and the soldiers bivouacked in tents around it. Living off the land, they killed Mr. Ciepelowicz's pigs and cows, but to my eternal regret, had no taste for goat meat. The farmyard became a slaughterhouse; they shot the animals, and Mr. Ciepelowicz, with my mother's help, skinned and quartered them. They wasted nothing. My mother made blood sausage and headcheese, while Mr. Ciepelowicz constructed a smokehouse to cure the hams and bacon. My mom was working eighteen-hour days. She was now cooking and cleaning, not only for us, but the entire officer corps.

She did such a superb job charming the Germans that it led to an unfortunate, dangerous, and bizarre situation. One of the younger officers fell in love with her and begged her to leave the farm for his parents' home in Germany, where she could spend the rest of the war in safety while she awaited his return. They took lengthy walks in the evening, and he told her how war-weary he was. He knew Germany was losing the war, and he wanted for it all to be over; he just wanted to survive. Sometimes he thought about "accidentally" shooting himself in the foot, so he could get out of what he now considered a doomed fight.

In retrospect, I often wondered whom this was harder on, my mother or my father. My Mom had to maintain the romantic illusion that kept the German a gentleman, instead of an officer in an all-conquering army who could force himself upon her. She played the grieving young widow, who wasn't yet ready to give herself to another man but admitted she found him attractive and promised to wait for his return from the war. But she insisted she had to stay on the farm. She had a responsibility to take care of her elderly aunt and uncle (the Ciepelowiczes); they were old and couldn't manage without her. They saved her, did so much for her, and took her and her poor child in after her husband died when she had no money and nowhere else to go. The officer, a sensitive soul, understood her dilemma and agreed to let her stay on the farm. He left head over heels in love with her, full of admiration for her unselfish nature.

My dad, in the meantime, had to stay in his room, helpless, playing the idiot while his wife was taking romantic walks with a man who could do whatever he wanted with her, and shoot him if he objected. I can just imagine the images of his wife embracing the German that coursed through his mind, and wondered how he controlled the rage seething within him. What did he say to her when she came back from the walks? Did he question her? Accuse her? Believe her? I never heard that part of the story, but often wondered whether his subsequent endless accusations of infidelity with every Tom, Dick, and Harry stemmed from that time.

We had to ignore the grotesque horror of this courtship, pretend it was normal even on days like the one when my mother's suitor came back from a patrol covered with blood. He told her he and his men ran into a group of Jews hiding in the woods who dared to defend themselves. They'd killed them, but he was furious, because the swine's blood ruined his uniform. My mother got him hot water so he could wash and calmed him down by promising to get the stains out. Throughout his stay, the besotted officer tried to score points with my mom by treating me as if I was already his son. He would ruffle my hair, give me candy, and offer to give me rides on his motorcycle. I accepted everything, feigned gratitude, and prayed the Russians killed him.

After a few weeks' stay, our occupiers picked up and left as suddenly as they'd arrived, retreating once more. During their stay, they never mistreated or even threatened us. They just took what they wanted and made it plain our role was to serve them. On one level, we knew that if we kowtowed to them and satisfied all their wishes, they wouldn't harm us, but we also knew what these friendly officers would do to us if they found out who we were. When they left, we could finally exhale; our sense of relief was so strong it was palpable. We survived once again, and while they ravaged the farm, we still had a roof over our heads, goats, chickens, and the vegetable garden, so there was no fear of going hungry, and life went back to normal.

A month after the Germans left, Mr. Ciepelowicz's younger brother and his wife arrived from Warsaw. They feared to stay there, expecting a prolonged and fierce battle, and came to the farm to wait out the end of the war in what they thought would be a safer place. They recognized we were Jewish and just smiled at our adamant denials. For the first time, however, we weren't worried, we could almost smell liberation and knew that even if they were so inclined, they were unlikely to report us to the Gendarmes for fear of hurting their brother, and sister-in-law who would be shot with us.

Soon after their arrival, they realized they had traded one dangerous place for another. Our farm, while isolated, was right in the middle of a strategic rectangle bounded on the long sides by a key highway and a rail line, and on the short sides by a bridge and a strategic road. The first inkling we were in the center of a battle zone were the sounds of heavy guns shooting over us. Those sounds got closer and louder from both directions, and we realized we needed to create a shelter. My father and the Ciepelowicz brothers dug a sloped hole about eight feet wide by twenty feet long and eight feet deep. They cut down a dozen huge trees, placed the trunks over the hole, and piled a couple feet of dirt over the trunks. They left a six-foot opening at the top of the slope to act as an entrance and/or exit.

A day or two after they finished the bunker, shells started falling close to the house, and we dashed to the shelter carrying whatever food and water we could snatch on the way out of the farmhouse. My parents and I had lots of practice being confined for lengthy periods of time in a gloomy underground space, but for the Ciepelowiczes, this was a new and excruciating experience. After a few hours, they tried to stretch their legs but retreated after venturing out just a few feet. Bullets and artillery shells were flying all over, and confinement, no matter how cramped, didn't seem so bad.

Each day, the battle grew in intensity and closeness. The noise deafened us, and we could feel the earth shake as bombs and shells exploded around us. We ran out of food and water after two days, so on the third day, my mother crawled out of the bunker, braved the bullets flying around her, and with her usual style, brought back not just food but a cooked meal.

Two days later, around two or three in the morning, Ciapek, who'd joined us in the bunker, barked his head off. We tried to shut him up, afraid his barking might alert a German patrol who'd mistake us for partisans, shoot first and not bother to ask questions later. We couldn't stop him. A flashlight blinded us, and a harsh, commanding, but thank God, non-Germanic voice yelled at us to come out. We didn't know what they wanted but crawled out of the bunker with our hands up. A half-dozen soldiers in grayish, dirty, and ill-fitting uniforms surrounded us; it was a Russian patrol reconnoitering behind enemy lines. The Russian language is a close enough relative of Polish and we explained we were locals, not Germans in disguise. In return, they told us they were a reconnaissance patrol sent out to probe the position of German lines. The long-prayed-for liberation day had arrived; our war was over.

The Ciepelowiczes remained in the bunker, unwilling to leave their farm, afraid someone might loot or vandalize it if they left it unguarded. We didn't want to risk falling into German hands again and went back with the Russians to safety and freedom. We hugged the Ciepelowiczes with genuine warmth and sadness. They treated us like family, never took a penny, and risked their lives out of fondness for my mother, and gratitude for the help she provided on the farm. No grandparents could have treated me better than they did. I am sorry I never got to see them again, but they'll always occupy a warm spot in my heart.

We followed the soldiers through the woods' silent shadows, too overcome to even know what to say or how to act. The day we had hoped and prayed for and sometimes doubted would ever come had arrived, but it was so different from the way we had imagined it. We dreamt about it for so long in our minds, it became like another long-awaited but fruitless hope for Jewish salvation: the coming of the Messiah. Such a memorable moment demanded the skies to open, at least a little, and was it asking too much for a few angels to blow their horns and announce the blessed event? I don't think so. Our liberation, like most things we ardently wish for in life, crept up on us with a whisper, instead of a grand entrance complete with fireworks and a brass band.

PART THREE
POLAND AFTER LIBERATION

7

Return to Wolomin

It was almost dawn when we arrived at the Russian encampment. To say it was spartan would be an understatement. Unlike the American army which worries about the soldiers' comfort and morale, the Russian army believed in minimalism when it came to creature comforts. The soldiers slept on the ground, out in the open, with no showers or any bathing facilities. They lived on a diet very similar to what we had become accustomed to during our stay in the cellar: bread, potatoes, occasional hot soup, and strong black tea.

We were so excited we couldn't sleep, but had eaten nothing all day, were starving, and we couldn't thank the cook enough who gave us some bread and tea with sugar. When the Russians found out we were Jewish, they led us to a major, a Russian Jew, who greeted us in Yiddish and wanted to know how we had survived. We talked for a while, but he had a war to fight, and we wanted to get back to Wolomin, which he told us was in liberated territory. We said goodbye and set off on foot along roads clogged with an endless stream of tanks and trucks moving in the opposite direction, towards the front. Diesel fumes spewing from exhausts fouled the air, but we didn't care. To us, it was the joyous smell of freedom and victory over the murderers who had tried to exterminate us like vermin.

We walked for days, stopped only at night wherever we found a Russian army encampment. They were very generous, sharing their meager meals of bread, tea, and potatoes with us. We slept on the ground in the open, feeling safe surrounded by the armed soldiers. We didn't dare spend the night on our own because, while we knew we were beyond the reach of the Germans, we feared we might get killed by some rogue segment of the Armja Krajowa, the Polish underground. Sometimes the roads became too crowded, and we had to walk through fields. This was sheer torture for me. I had outgrown my shoes and the protruding stubs from harvested wheat stalks bit into my bare feet like nails. We persevered, and after nine or ten days, arrived in Wolomin, our hometown where my parents expected to pick up their life where they'd left off five years ago.

We reoccupied the downstairs of our old house, the Baginskis, the old couple who had sold my parents the house and the store before the war, continued to live upstairs. The store shelves were empty, all the goods sold, stolen, or confiscated during our absence, and no one offered to either return or pay for them. It didn't matter; we had survived, and my mom was now free to operate in the open. She was a wonder to behold. Not only did she have her previous boundless energy, but now, armed with a total disdain for the law and when necessary, the truth, she was unstoppable. The law didn't protect us during the war, and she felt no obligations towards it. Where were all these law-abiding moralists when we needed them? For the rest of her life, she saw the law only as a problem that a clever person, such as herself, could overcome or get around to get what she needed to earn a living.

There was a shortage of everything, and she became an expert at getting people what they needed. Her most successful deals involved soldiers from the Asian Soviet republics. These were tough warriors and came from rural areas in backward regions of Russian Central Asia, still entrenched in the Middle Ages. They were illiterate and seemed to have only two uses for books and newspapers: as toilet tissues and for rolling tobacco into cigarettes. They were fond of vodka and prized watches above all else. For them, a watch was the ultimate status symbol, a mark of culture and sophistication. They thought watches were magic wonders, and since they had no clue of how they worked, assumed bigger was better. My mother was not one to disabuse them of that concept. In her first coup she traded an old three-legged alarm clock with a bell on top she had equipped with a jerry-rigged watchband to a Kalmuk for a truck he had captured from the Germans. I'll never forget the look on his face as he strutted out of our store. His chest puffed out and his head held high, proud to wear a clock the size of a large grapefruit on his wrist. He came back furious the next day, threatened to kill my mother for selling him a defective watch. When he woke up in the morning, the clock had stopped ticking, and his mates made fun of him for letting a woman cheat him. It took several glasses of vodka and a lesson on how to wind the clock, to pacify him and send him back proud and elated to his regiment.

Afterwards, the rest of his outfit besieged my mother. They all wanted a big watch like their buddy, and she was more than willing to accommodate them. They didn't have money, but they offered to barter to get her anything she wanted in trade. Not being an intrusive person, she never inquired into how or where they found the things they brought her. Only once was she unable to avoid knowing the obvious provenance of one of the trade items. There was a shortage of leather and she had put it on a list of items she would accept for one of her wondrous large watches. The next day, the town lost all electrical power. The big leather belt on the local electrical generator disappeared during the night. No one knew how. My mother had leather for sale, and another proud Kalmuk was sporting an alarm clock on his wrist.

Sometimes the soldiers' lack of understanding of watches took strange and even dangerous turns. One day, two soldiers came to the store carrying a grandfather clock. They realized it was too big to carry as a personal watch and came up with what to them was an obvious and logical solution. They wanted my mother to cut it up into twenty or thirty smaller watches, which they could send back home or sell to others. When my mother told them it was impossible, they thought it was a trick. She was trying to cheat them, and they threatened to shoot her if she didn't do what they wanted. Worn out from dragging the heavy clock, they didn't want their dreams destroyed. They were ignorant, but armed, angry, and dangerous. It took all my mother's skill to diffuse their anger and resolve the problem. After plying them with vodka, she confessed they were right, but only a skilled watchmaker, which she was not, knew how to cut up a clock. She liked them; they seemed like nice guys, so she would help them. She knew a good watchmaker in Warsaw who, when their outfit got there, would perform this delicate operation at a reasonable price, especially if they mentioned her name. Mollified by my mother's confession and many glasses of vodka, they stumbled off happy, dragging their mother of all "watches," clutching the fake name and address, arguing how many watches the watchmaker would produce from the clock and how rich they would become.

The large watch business was only one of my mother's money-making activities. The business plan she developed in these early days after liberation was one she stuck with splendid success for the rest of her life. Unlike the pre-war years when my parents ran a bicycle, sports-goods, and radio shop, she refused to tie herself down to specific products or commodities. She learned from bitter experience that in time of crisis, your assets must always be liquid and portable, so she never allowed herself to build up inventory. All transactions involved a rapid movement of goods from a supplier to a consumer, passing through her hands just long enough to leave a residual profit. If circumstances didn't lend themselves to this kind of deal, she was not above helping the process along by creating an appearance of demand when burdened with unwanted supply.

A case in point was her adventure into the wonderful world of yeast. For some strange reason, while we lived with a shortage of everything else, there was an oversupply of yeast, and my mother bought a truckload at a fire sale price. Having assured a supply, she set about creating demand. She paid a stranger, who was passing through, to visit the yeast dealers in town, present himself as a representative of a large bakery in Warsaw who was looking for a truckload of yeast. Price was not an issue, but he didn't want any partial quantities. It had to be a full truckload or nothing. He had to be back in Warsaw the next day and would check that evening whether any dealer could fill his order. Later in the day, my mother spread the news she had a truckload of yeast. After lengthy negotiations, during which she cursed the dealers for trying to take advantage of her because she was just a poor woman, she gave in, and agreed to sell the yeast at a "pitiful" price, which left her with a very handsome profit. She commiserated with the dealers when the out-of-town buyer never showed up and shared with them her opinion of Warshawers, city people, who were just a bunch of big talking, unreliable phonies.

While my parents were trying to reestablish themselves, I was paying the price for being isolated from children all those years. An overachiever, even at such an early age, I tried to catch up to my peers by coming down with every childhood disease known to man. Whooping cough, measles, rubella, scarlet fever--you name it, I had it all within a few months period. The final straw that almost broke the proverbial camel's back was diphtheria. The previous illnesses depleted me and the local pharmacy, which was short of everything, lacked the medication I needed. I was running a very high fever, hallucinating most of the time, and the local doctor doubted I would survive it. Lucky for me, God gifted me with a sturdy little peasant body, and a resourceful mother. I don't know how she found out the antitoxin I needed was available in a town thirty miles away, or whom she bribed to go get it for her. There was no public transportation, the war was still going on, and thirty miles might as well have been a thousand. Only the army had the means to get the medicine and return in time before I became too ill to recover. I assume she paid off some Russian soldier with a truck with her usual currency, vodka, or maybe even one of her famous large watches. The exact details do not really matter, the medicine arrived, and to my parents' delight and the doctor's surprise, I recovered and in a few weeks was as good as new.

When they were sure I had given up my attempts to get into the Guinness book of World Records for most illnesses in the shortest length of time, my parents decided it was time for me to begin my formal education. They had home-schooled me while we were hiding out at the Pashnicks. I knew how to read, write, and do simple arithmetic, but my going to school was a symbol of a return to normalcy, reclaiming old hopes, asserting a belief in a future. So, on a day I am not likely to forget, nervously clutching a book bag filled with a notebook, a bottle of ink, a pen, some pencils, an eraser, and a ruler, I followed my parents to the local school.

After proving I could read and write, they enrolled me for my shortest stay in any educational institution. Everything was fine while we were in class but, when we were let out for recess, my male classmates surrounded me. After calling me the usual witty, original names-Judas, Caiaphas, dirty Jew, Christ killer-they pummeled me until the school bell announced the end of recess. I tried to defend myself, determined to ignore my parents' instructions to accept the beating or wait till my assailants became bored or tired. I refused to be the traditional passive, long suffering Jew; look where it got us, straight into the gas chambers. I wanted to be like the heroes of the Warsaw ghetto who died fighting for their dignity. However, I was both outnumbered and unskilled in the art of fighting, or anything that relied on physical strength.

I didn't bother going back to the classroom. I knew they would repeat beating me at every opportunity, and the teacher who had watched it all without intervening would not protect me, so I picked myself up and went home. My parents were shocked to see the state I was in when I returned home. The boys tore my clothes; I had a black eye, a bloody nose, and assorted bruises. Every part of my body ached, but mixed with the pain and anger at my tormentors there was a warm glow of pride. I had not run scared like a traditional Jew; they may have creamed me, but at least I had fought back. Though it had been by Pyrrhic standards a tiny moral victory, I saw it as a first step in overcoming two thousand years of Jewish self-emasculation.

There were two or three thousand Jews in Wolomin before the war, but we were the only ones who returned. I don't know how many survived but went elsewhere, or returned after we left town, but at that time we were it. My less than enthusiastic reception in school was only one of many clues our fellow townspeople were not overjoyed to have us back in their midst. People who had known my parents for years ignored them on the street and would only speak to them when they needed something my mother, in her entrepreneurial way, could get them.

The fact my parents owned our house and store, and paid hard cash for it, counted for nothing. The Poles, who had taken it over after the Nazis sent us to the ghetto, felt they were the true owners. They had expected we would die like the rest of the Jews. To have to vacate the premises when we returned, seemed like another example of how the "greedy Shylocks" were always extracting their pound of flesh from righteous Gentiles.

The Zarembas, outraged by our refusal to share our "hidden treasure" with them, further fueled resentment. It didn't excuse my mother's desperate though still dishonest ploy, but it helped assuage whatever little guilt she may have felt when the Baginskis, our upstairs tenants, told her strange intruders kept digging up the back garden at night for months on end. My mother, never one to miss an opportunity to emote and tie up loose ends, seized upon this bit of useful information with her usual gusto. She ran to the Zarembas' house, tearing her hair and crying, "We're ruined! We're ruined! Everything's gone! Hooligans dug up the treasure while we were hiding. The Baginskis saw them but were too old and feeble to stop them." The Zarembas didn't believe her but couldn't accuse her of lying and holding out on them, without having to admit they'd been the ones digging behind her back. So, they said nothing to her but spewed venom about us to whoever would listen.

We never learned why the local Armja Krajowa planned to proceed with its own version of ethnic cleansing. For all we knew it could have just been old habits dying hard, but once we found out, through one of my mother's many more or less shady contacts, we knew we had to leave town. We spent the next three nights sleeping in the Russian army barracks. The local Russian commander was Jewish. He put an armed guard at our front door and announced he would show no mercy to anyone who tried to harm us. We gathered our few meager possessions and set off for Warsaw on an army truck.

8

Warsaw

Warsaw was just one big ruin with only a few houses still standing. The Germans destroyed the ghetto during the uprising. It was a substantial section of the city that housed almost half a million Jews before the war. They devastated the rest of the city during the battle for its liberation. The Armja Krajowa rose up against the German garrison as soon as the Russians approached the outskirts of the city. They expected the Russians to attack and wanted to take part in liberating the Polish capital. For some strange reason, the Russians waited in the suburbs while the battle between the Polish underground and the Germans raged for days, block-by-block, house-by-house. Many Poles believed the Russians stood by and watched because they wanted the Germans to decimate the right-wing Partisans, likely future opponents of the communist government they planned to install after the war. When they moved in, the city was just a pile of rubble.

Since there was no place to live in Warsaw proper, we moved into a one-room apartment in Praga, which was a suburb or a borough of Warsaw. A small sink supplied cold water, and every few days my mother used it to wash our one set of underwear. She cooked our meals on a portable two-burner gas stove, and since we had no table or chairs, we ate sitting on the bed, holding the plates on our laps. There was no need for dressers. We had no clothes besides the ones we wore on our backs. The toilet, the usual two-stepper, was in the hall, and serviced the six or seven apartments on our floor.

Despite the cramped conditions, we adapted to life in Warsaw. Many Jewish survivors gathered there, and they were determined to reconstitute a functioning Jewish community, complete with a synagogue, a Jewish council, and a Beit Din (Jewish court). My father became a member of the council while my mother went looking for ways to make a buck, and boy, did she ever find them!

The entire business establishment was in a state of chaos; there was no organized system for the transportation and distribution of goods. There were shortages of certain commodities in one part of the country, while mountains of the same rotted next to idle railroad tracks only fifty miles away. This was a perfect climate for making money on the black market. Somehow, my mother found people and trucks who helped her move merchandise from areas of surplus where she could buy them at very low prices to areas of scarcity where she could sell them at a premium. Often, our one-room apartment served as a temporary warehouse for whatever was the transaction du jour: medicines, hams, tires, furs, condoms, yes, condoms. Mom brought a truckload of them from Germany and sold them at a very handsome profit to drugstores in Warsaw. Condoms were in short supply in Poland and were much needed to control venereal diseases spread by both the German and Russian armies.

Besides tangible goods, my mother branched out into trading foreign currencies, as well as gold and diamonds on the black market. This was an even more profitable sideline and didn't require any overhead. None of the surviving Jews trusted the Polish zloty and, like my parents, they all learned it was important to have liquid, portable assets. Everyone was converting their zlotys into foreign currency, preferably U.S. dollars, and, since you couldn't buy foreign money from a bank, the black market became the only game in town. The unofficial money market operated just like a stock exchange, the price of U.S. dollars, British pounds, Dutch guilders, Russian gold five-ruble pieces better known as piggies, fluctuated daily and sometimes even hourly, based on supply and demand. However, some irrational criteria shaped by ignorance and local urban myths affected prices.

Daniel Kahneman won the 2002 Nobel Prize in economics for showing that rational markets make systematic, irrational errors that affect prices and create market inefficiencies exploited by clever arbitrageurs. Almost sixty years earlier, my mother, with only a fourth-grade education, unable to even spell arbitrageur, intuitively understood the concept, and as usual, used it to her advantage. There was a significant difference in the price of different dollar bills. Older, longer bills sold for five to ten percent less than their normal size newer counterparts. However, for some unknown reason, traders believed 1928-dollar bills with a round orange watermark were more valuable and they sold at a five to ten percent premium. My mother was the only one who recognized this was nonsense, dollars were dollars, and she made an under the table deal with an official of JOINT, a Jewish American charitable organization, to exchange long for short dollars at a one percent premium, and two percent if he gave her the prized 1928's. This transaction was profitable for the official who was more than happy to cooperate, but it was a gold mine for my mom, who bought up all the long dollars she could get on the market.

Currency dealers made only a small commission on each sale, but the volume of business was so large it was a very profitable enterprise. The key to success was to avoid getting stuck with a large inventory of foreign currency in a price downturn. Therefore, Mom acted only as a middle woman. I became very useful to her as a courier. Most days, I would pick up a load of foreign currency from one dealer and carry it in a book bag to another. It was a brilliant ploy. What police officer would suspect a scrawny, eight-year-old ragamuffin in patched clothes, was carrying a small fortune on his back? My only fear was some Polish boys would attack me and steal my bag to torment a Jewish kid.

I wore patched clothes because they were the ones I wore when we escaped the ghetto. Mom kept them together with a needle, thread, and a prayer. Ever practical, she bought my clothes several sizes too big before we went into the ghetto. By now they were not only threadbare, but I was also busting out of them. However, times being what they were, nobody thought about going shopping as long as the clothes held together. I kept wearing them because we lived in an era of low personal indulgence.

In between courier jobs, I spent my time daydreaming, a habit I had honed into an art during our years in the cellar. This time, however, both my body and my mind were free to roam. I wandered through the streets of Praga fantasizing about fighting the Germans with the Palestine brigade, the Jewish regiment from Palestine who fought with Montgomery in the African campaign against Rommel. A Jewish brigade! Jewish soldiers in uniform! Carrying guns! Fighting! Who had ever heard of such a thing? This was even better than the Warsaw ghetto rebellion. It proved Jews would fight even when they weren't desperate and had nothing left to lose. This was so different from everything my parents taught me about what Jews were and weren't, did and didn't do. That there was such a thing as the Palestine Brigade meant maybe you didn't have to be meek if you were Jewish. Fighting back instead of running away didn't make you one of "Them," a soulless brute. In my fantasies, I was a member of the brigade, and we kicked some serious German ass.

After a few months in Warsaw, my parents decided it was time to make another attempt to expose me to formal education. Warsaw was a metropolis, not a provincial small town. The people in Warsaw, they thought, were more sophisticated and, while they might be anti-

Semitic, they expected them to be gentler. The students might shun or harass me with the usual insults reserved for Jews, but they wouldn't assault and beat me up like the kids in Wolomin. They were wrong. My classmates ignored me during the day but caught up with me on the way home. They beat me and left me bruised and bleeding in the snow. I spent a few days in bed to recover from the beating, proving once and for all that I would not flourish in the Polish educational system.

9

A Tale of Two Orphanages

My parents didn't want to postpone my education any longer. They understood it wasn't normal for an eight-year-old to spend his time being a little adult. They concluded the only place I could go to school and hang out with other kids without losing life or limb was a Jewish orphanage. There were several set up by HIAS (Hebrew International Aid Society) for Jewish children who'd survived the war hidden by righteous Gentiles. My parents picked the one in Zatrzebie and sent me off on a truck along with some merchandise my mom was sending to a neighboring town.

We arrived at the orphanage late at night; I was hungry, tired, and a little scared. Two men in their forties greeted me and told me the dining room was closed; they hoped I could wait until breakfast. They didn't offer an alternative, so I assured them I could, and they took me to the boy's dormitory. It looked like an enormous hospital ward, pristine and clean, filled with metal folding beds arranged in rows. They put on the light long enough to lead me to my assigned bed and left after putting out the light and closing the door. I started undressing in the dark; exhausted, I couldn't wait to get into bed and fall asleep. It was around midnight, and everyone was supposed to be asleep, but as soon as the sound of the adults' steps died out, the entire room came to life. A dozen flashlights dispelled the darkness. Forty to fifty boys of all ages surrounded me and examined me from all angles. They bombarded me with abrupt, unfriendly questions.

"What's your name?"

"Mietek."

"Where are you from?"

"Warsaw."

"How old are you?"

"Eight."

"Do you think you can beat Chrzaszcz (Beetle)?"

"Who is Chrzaszcz? I don't know anyone named Chrzaszcz."

"That's Chrzaszcz, over there." My interlocutor, a burly teenager, pointed towards a scrawny little boy who hovered on the edge of the group. "Can you beat him?"

"I don't know. Why does it matter? I don't want to fight him."

"Well, you're going to."

The boys grabbed me and pushed me in the middle of a circle of excited and hooting boys, face to face with poor Chrzaszcz who seemed even more scared and less eager to fight than I. There was no escape; we pushed and grappled with each other and fell to the ground with me on top. Chrzaszcz stopped struggling, and the biggest boy declared me the winner. I got up and tried to make my way towards my bed.

"Where do you think you're going?"

"To bed. I want to go to sleep."

"No, you don't, now you fight Zhaba (Frog)."

There was no point arguing; I was back in the center of the circle, facing a bigger and much more aggressive opponent. The surrounding crowd made no bones about who was their favorite. They cheered on their homeboy, urging him to beat the crap out of the new kid. Scared, homesick, and alone, I wanted to cry. But filled with rage at my tormentors, I refused to satisfy their desire to see me humiliated and threw myself at Zhaba with far more vigor than I'd used with poor Chrzaszcz. I fought him with determination and ardor fueled by anger, but he was bigger, stronger, and a far more experienced fighter. After a few minutes, he had me down, sat on my chest, and pummeled my face. Misio (Bear), the biggest boy and unquestioned leader of the group, stopped the fight. He declared Zhaba the winner, and at last allowed me to crawl into bed, where I fell asleep after sobbing quietly; I didn't want the bastards to know they had gotten to me.

Years later, studying Group Dynamics, I realized the boys weren't interested in humiliating me. The ordeal wasn't personal; it was necessary. The boys had to determine where I fit in their hierarchy, and since strength defined rank, you were who you could beat. The next morning, they treated me like a normal member of the gang. They expected me to defer to everyone other than poor Chrzaszcz, but there was very little bullying. Misio ran a benevolent dictatorship and didn't tolerate any unnecessary meanness. After a few days, as an ultimate sign of acceptance, they gave me my orphanage name, Słoń (elephant), pronounced Swogne in Polish. The nicknames were the only names used and were very perceptive descriptions of an individual's attributes or personality. They called Misio the bear because of his strength. Zhaba had bulging eyes and looked a lot like a frog, and I, because of the years of confinement in the cellar, moved slowly and deliberately like an elephant.

Zatrzebie was the Waldorf Astoria of orphanages, set on a beautiful old estate with extensive grounds and majestic old trees. It had three main buildings: a two-story boys' house with the dormitory on the top and administration offices on the ground floor, a separate and smaller girls' dormitory, and a large one-story structure with French doors on all sides that served as both dining room and lounge. There was a separate compact building with a dozen showers where we bathed every Saturday. This was my first exposure to showers. What an improvement over dabbing your body with a wet rag dipped in a small basin of hot water. You could wash your complete body and be clean. The most amazing part of the shower, believe it or not, was the soap. After a lifetime of washing with gritty, rock-hard, brown lumps, we were all awed by Ivory soap; it was so white, soft, and foamy. Ivory soap became for us a metaphor for America, a place where everything was so much easier, better, and more refined.

I remember little about the staff at Zatrzebie, composed of Polish Jews. They took excellent care of our physical needs but had no real impact on our everyday life. I don't know what happened on the girls' side. We only met them during meals, but the only thing that mattered to the boys was what Misio said or wanted. That is why only the interactions with my fellow inmates remain etched in my memory.

For the first time in years, I had other kids to play with. The food was excellent. I got new clothes that fit, there were plenty of books, and I even went to school for a month or two. It was in a one-room schoolhouse where, for the first time, I experienced a structured school setting. I can't say school thrilled me. It was all right, but given a choice, I preferred reading just for the hell of it, paying attention only to what interested me. I can't say my preferences have changed much since then.

Several months passed without a word from my parents. I missed them and wondered if I would ever see them again. Some days I let the ugly thought they'd abandoned me and would never come back to get me creep into my mind, but I repressed it; it was too painful to accept. However, as months passed and I heard nothing from them, I started feeling as much of an orphan as the others. My parents were alive, but for all intents and purposes, they were as absent from my life as my roommates' dead parents were from theirs.

The last stroke of irony that certified my official status as a pseudo-orphan was the picture taken with a big shot, Harry Schwartz, the president of HIAS. He was making a tour of Poland to assess both needs and how the various institutions spent the money raised by his organization. During his visit to Zatrzebie, the photographer accompanying him wanted a picture of our benefactor with his hand on the shoulder of a grateful orphan. He picked me. I was one of the youngest and looked appropriately waiflike. The picture appeared on the front page of The Forward, the leading Jewish newspaper in New York, and I'm sure it helped raise consciousness and money for Jewish orphans in Europe. By a stroke of luck the photographer, Mietek Wyszogrod, later became one of my mother's best friends and gave me a copy after we met at her funeral.

After a while, I started hearing rumors from the older boys that my parents were in jail. I tried to ignore them, and assumed their comments were just mean-spirited taunts. However, part of me wanted to believe them. Being in jail would explain why my parents didn't come to visit. I preferred having criminal parents to being abandoned. The boys turned out to be right. One day, I was told to report to the administrative office -- my parents were there to see me. I ran faster than I'd ever run before, more gazelle than elephant. After hugging them, I realized something was different. A kerchief covered my mother's head, but it was easy to see she had no hair.

They'd been in prison, where the jailers shaved my mother's head. I was very young, but even then, I knew what a blow this must have been. Any woman would feel violated by having her head shaved, but few were as conscious of their looks as my mom. It wasn't just vanity, though God knows she had more than her share of that. Her physical appearance was an important asset, a tool she used to gain an edge on and charm foolish men, a description that in her estimation covered the whole male species. Her hair shorn like Samson's, she lost power and felt vulnerable, not a comfortable state for someone who saw life as a permanent guerilla war.

The police arrested my parents for black marketing, on a tip from my mother's cousin Moishe. My mother had used him to help her move merchandise, and he was unhappy with his share of the profits. With my parents out of the way in jail, he convinced the janitor, who knew he was a relative, to let him into the apartment. Once there, he ransacked the place until he found their money hidden in the false bottom of a dresser drawer. The police released my parents on bail put up by one of my mother's gentile partners. These generous people ran a jewelry store my mother supplied with watches smuggled from Switzerland. They were very fond of her and put up the bail, even though they knew my parents were likely to leave Poland rather than go back to prison, and they would lose the bail money.

Imagine my parents' despair when they came home. The dresser drawer was empty. Someone had absconded with the twenty thousand dollars, a minor fortune in those days that they had worked so hard to accumulate. Once again, they'd lost everything and were penniless. They took Moishe to the Beit Din, the informal Jewish court. He denied stealing the money, and even though the circumstantial evidence was overwhelming, no one had seen him do it. They couldn't force him to give back money he swore he didn't have. No one believed him, and the whole Jewish community shunned him. It reflected the mores of the times that they shunned him for being an informer; stealing was a more easily forgivable act, although it would have been in better taste if he had stolen from a gentile.

My parents came to Zatrzebie to tell me their plans for our future. They couldn't stay in Poland; with Moishe the shameless goniff (thief) as a witness, they knew they'd lose in court and wind up with a stiff jail sentence. They planned to escape to Germany and stay in a displaced persons' camp until they could get to Palestine. In the meantime, they were sending me to an orphanage in Lodz. They felt I would be better off and have a more stable environment in an orphanage than on the run with "fugitives from justice." The Haganah, the underground

Jewish army in Palestine, planned to smuggle the children in my new orphanage into Palestine, and I later found out they wound up on the ship Exodus whose story Leon Uris described in his book of that name. According to their plan, we would reunite in Eretz Israel (the Holy Land) and never separate again. I preferred to go with my parents. From my point of view, they, not an orphanage, represented stability. But I had no choice, so I kissed them goodbye and got ready for the new, unknown experience.

I put "fugitives from justice" in quotations because my parents never felt they were criminals. They didn't think they had done anything wrong; they didn't hurt anyone but were just trying to make a living, and considering the times, I couldn't agree with them more. The Jews, coming back from hiding places and German concentration camps or Russian gulags, spent five years doing whatever it took to survive. Relentless, unjust, and immoral regimes pursued them. During that time, the laws of the land not only didn't protect them, they often victimized them. Now the war was over and they expected them to act as if nothing had happened. They had to obey the laws in which they had no faith, and for which they had lost all respect.

The next day, late at night, I boarded the back of a truck going to Lodz. The only other passenger was a girl named Anya, who was also going to the new orphanage. Anya was about my age and beautiful, with a round rosy face, a head full of blond curls, and bright blue eyes. She looked more like a stereotypical Polish girl than a Jewish orphan. We knew each other by sight but had never spoken to each other because the orphanage kept boys and girls separate. It was dark outside as the truck sped through the countryside; I felt lonely and afraid of what awaited me in Lodz. Somehow, without a word being exchanged between us or even a conscious decision, we wound up next to each other on the narrow metal bench, holding hands. We never said a word the entire night, but pressed our bodies together like newborn puppies, finding comfort and solace in the feel of each other's presence. We never let go of each other's hand until they separated us at the orphanage, and we never saw each other again. I would catch glimpses of her as boys and girls rushed past each other on the way from one activity to another. We never had a chance even to stand still together in the same room.

I think sometimes about Anya and that night. She represents my one perfect relationship with another human being. We gave each other comfort and emotional support, with no hidden agendas or scorekeeping. Maybe only children can be so generous, or maybe we were lucky. We didn't have enough time together to screw it up by being human and, therefore, fallible. Anyway, Anya old girl (by now old is an appropriate term for both of us), here is looking at you, kid! After all, we'll always have the truck.

The new orphanage differed from Zatrzebie. Instead of a hundred kids allowed to roam in a spacious and pastoral setting, the Lodz orphanage had over two hundred orphans stuffed into a four-story building in the heart of a major industrial city. Small metal cots filled every square inch of space; they squeezed my bed along with two others under the second-floor stairs. Six other cots faced us along the landing's wall.

The place was a beehive of activity. Unlike Zatrzebie, adults and not inmates ran the orphanage and imposed a rigorous schedule of activities. The staff intended to deprogram overnight centuries of training in meekness and passivity and turn submissive Jews into proud Zionists worthy of living in and fighting for the Promised Land. We had intensive Hebrew lessons and impassioned lectures on Zionism, the new religion. Our reward would come not in heaven, but right here on earth in the paradise called Palestine. We sang Hatikvah, the Israeli national anthem, at every opportunity; the first time I heard it I was so thrilled that the hair on the back of my neck stood up, my eyes filled with tears, and for a moment I couldn't breathe. Somehow a national anthem proved we weren't just a ragtag bunch of gypsies the goyim could sneer at and abuse. We were a real nation with our own land and, yes, our own fucking real national anthem. Growing up in America, you think of yourself as an American who is Jewish. It may be hard for an American Jew to understand how it feels to be treated as a despised outsider. How I longed for a place where I was not just tolerated. A place where if I wanted to be an asshole, I could tell others to go back to where *they* came from.

Most of the kids in the orphanage had been together for several months and bonded through the intense indoctrination in Zionism, and most of them spoke rudimentary Hebrew. In this institution, they ranked you based on how much you had progressed towards the ideal new Jew, a Palestinian, not one whom you could beat. Once again, I felt I was sucking hind tit. I felt excluded by my lack of shared knowledge and despaired of ever catching up. You can't imagine my joy when they called me to the office and told me my parents changed their mind about us journeying separately to Israel. In fact, they changed their minds and now planned to emigrate to America.

10

Fleeing Poland

A truck took me to Katowice, an industrial city in Western Poland, where I rejoined my parents. We stayed there for three days with some acquaintances while my parents made travel arrangements. Our goal was West Germany, where we planned to stay in a Displaced Persons or DP camp. Hundreds of thousands of Jews lived there, sometimes for two or three years, while they waited for visas out of Europe or a ship that would smuggle them into Israel. Everybody wanted to go to America, but the American quota for Eastern Europeans was tiny, and after a while most settled for any place that would take them. Many of our relatives and acquaintances wound up in Canada, Australia, Argentina, Uruguay, and even South Africa.

My parents feared getting arrested by the police and going back to jail, for God knows how long. We had to get out of Poland before they caught us. They couldn't find direct passage into West Germany; the best they got were false papers and train tickets to Czechoslovakia. Three days after I rejoined them, we got on the train, the first step on our lengthy journey away from the killing fields.

After a lengthy train ride, we arrived in Prague and moved into a DP camp on the edge of town. The camp was not just dreary but downright depressing, even by our undemanding standards. It consisted of several very large army-type wooden barracks clustered in the center of a barren piece of land surrounded by barbed wire. I don't remember a single tree, bush, or blade of grass on the entire property. Even weeds, which grow anywhere, refused to take root in this desolate soil. We ate in shifts in one barrack that served as a communal dining room. A small, three-room building served as the infirmary, and the rest of the barracks served as sleeping quarters. I say sleeping rather than living quarters, because you didn't want to spend a minute more than you had to there. Our barrack was half the width and length of a football field, filled with triple-decker metal bunk beds with straw-filled mattresses lined up in tight rows. There were four sinks and four toilets, shielded from public view by a plywood wall, at each end of the barrack: one for women, the other for men. Each barrack housed several hundred people; there was no space to move, and we had to stand in endless lines to clean ourselves or use the toilets. Despite these overcrowded conditions, I don't remember any fights or even any bitter arguments. We were all accustomed to meager accommodations, and knew, or at least hoped, that this was only a temporary way station. Plans and hopes for the future sustained us and helped us ignore our depressing surroundings.

Staying in the barracks during the day was impossible. There was no space and nothing to do in camp, so every day we took a bus into Prague to see the city and check with Jewish aid organizations on options for getting further on our way. Prague was beautiful; unlike Warsaw, it survived the war unscathed. We wandered through the medieval part of town, including the ancient Ghetto, where we found the synagogue of the famous Rabbi Loew who created the Golem, an early Frankenstein he molded out of clay to protect the Jews of Prague during the Middle Ages. The town had beautiful wide boulevards and grand old bridges that spanned the Vltava. We admired all the bridges but favored one with a metal arch covered with a Hebrew inscription in huge golden letters. We used a funicular railway to visit the Hradcyn castle perched on a steep hill over the city. The old castle was majestic and dramatic, but what I enjoyed the most were the magnificent gardens descending from it towards town.

Even considering the accommodations, I enjoyed our stay in Prague. The only unpleasant memory of our month in the camp was my impromptu tonsillectomy. I am not sure why my parents decided I should have my tonsils removed, but one sunny morning, bribed into a state of only mild hysteria by promises of a cornucopia of post-operational ice cream, they led, or more accurately dragged, me into the infirmary. The doctor operated a cappella, without anesthetic. My parents gripped me while the surgeon forced my mouth wide open by holding my nose. He shoved something that looked like a long and narrow ice cream scoop down my throat. After what seemed like hours, but was more likely closer to a minute, he withdrew the scoop and declared the operation a success. I was in pain, spitting blood and fury; to my parents' shock and amazement I proceeded, between sobs, to show the richness of my vocabulary. I discoursed at great length not only on the dubious legitimacy of the doctor's birth and the morality, or rather the lack thereof, of every one of his female relatives going back to Eve, I suggested his sexual interest in canines smacked of unrepressed oedipal tendencies. This venting didn't reduce the physical pain, but it was satisfying; I had learned more at Zatrzebie than I had realized. Without my stay there, my performance could never have reached such rhetorical and linguistic heights.

I recovered for three days in the infirmary, feeling betrayed as only a nine-year-old can; my parents didn't come through with even one of the promised thousand ice cream cones. I didn't care that there was no ice cream stand within ten miles of camp. They had promised me ice cream as a payoff for undergoing (in my mind) an unnecessary trauma; trustworthy parents would have kept their promise.

While I was in the infirmary, a fake cable from the French State Department in Paris arrived at the French embassy in Prague, authorizing five thousand visas for war refugees. The next morning, thousands of Jews, including my parents, who discovered a burning desire to experience Gallic culture, lined up at the embassy. When I came out of the infirmary, we packed our belongings into a small valise and took the train to Paris.

PART FOUR
PARIS

11

Hotel Francia

We arrived in Paris's Gare de Lyon early in the morning. My parents suspected the French government, once it realized the Czech embassy issued the visas without its permission, would expel all bearers of the illegitimate documents. They also knew of France's tradition of welcoming political dissenters. Therefore, eager to show proper manners, they accommodated our hosts' preferences, discarded our visas, and declared themselves political refugees, escapees of a repressive communist regime.

Once processed through immigration, we went outside the railroad station to wait with other refugees for representatives from HIAS who would provide us with lodging. The folks from HIAS may not have conspired in sending the fake telegram, but they were aware of it, and prepared to accommodate the sudden onslaught of Jewish Francophiles.

HIAS was a visible and legal part of a loose and extensive network of Jewish aid. Money from American Jews and a deep belief we had to help each other, because no one else would, fueled it. The world's indifference to the Jewish plight during the war convinced the Jewish community that, when the chips were down, we could only depend on ourselves. The network provided myriad services, both legal and otherwise. It founded orphanages, fed, clothed, and lodged hundreds of thousands in and out of camps, provided job training, and set up registries of survivors to help reunite families separated by the war. It also smuggled arms and settlers into Palestine, set up clandestine training camps in France for the prospective Israeli army (the Haganah), and provided false papers for the ever-westward-moving Jewish flood.

While we waited for transportation, I saw my first black person, a Zouave, a soldier in one of France's more colorful African regiments. His blue-black skin looked even darker against his exotic bright red uniform. I had read about Negroes but wasn't sure they existed in real life and weren't just a literary fantasy; Eastern Europe at the time was not a hotbed of diversity. Czechoslovakia was the only foreign country I had visited, and though more westernized and sophisticated, it was still Slavic and its culture and population were similar to Poland's. I took the sight of the colorful African as an omen. We were now in a different and far more exotic land; I couldn't wait to see more.

After a brief wait, the HIAS representatives loaded us onto buses and took us to the organization's offices where we registered, received ration books and coupons for meals at the free soup kitchen, and a voucher for a residential hotel. This being France, the ration books covered the obvious necessities of life, such as wine, cigarettes, and cheese. My parents always sold the ration stamps for wine and cigarettes, but kept the coupons for cheese, which at first led to a rather bitter cultural misunderstanding. They bristled when a grocer tried to sell them Camembert and Brie, cheeses which, to their experienced eyes, had gone bad. They might be new in France, and had fallen on hard times, but they weren't stupid, and nobody would put anything over on them. In time, they learned the French weren't trying to dupe them - they liked their cheese moldy and runny. This only reinforced my parents' low opinion of our hosts; they saw them as childish and frivolous people who frittered away their money on strange food, smoking, wine, and sex. The war stomped out whatever playfulness ever lived in my parents' souls. There was no room for frivolity in their worldview, and they couldn't understand wasting money on pleasure. Money -- liquid portable money, not stationary assets like houses, furniture, or cars -- was the only valuable commodity and the ultimate source of security.

HIAS assigned us lodging at the Hotel Francia, which became our home for the next three years. Hotel Francia was at 20 rue du Vertbois in the 3rd Arrondissement. Rue du Vertbois means the street of green woods, which was a misnomer if I ever saw one. While Paris is replete with wonderful parks and numberless streets lined with majestic trees, rue du Vertbois isn't one of them. It was four or five blocks of asphalt and cement, devoid of even a blade of grass. The neighborhood is now undergoing serious gentrification, but at the time we lived there it comprised two small hotels, the College Turgot (a high school), a grocery store, a bakery, and a pharmacy, the rest were shabby four and five story, narrow apartment houses. A mixture of French and Algerian working-class people inhabited the street; the two groups coexisted but refused to socialize with each other.

Hotel Francia had five floors and a very narrow façade but was deep. The owner, Monsieur Habib, an old, crippled, retired Lebanese pimp, lived like a mole in a dark apartment on the first floor with his much younger Arab girlfriend, Yvonne. My mother shunned her and would only deal with Monsieur Habib. I always suspected it was because of her belief she had an edge when she dealt with men, but she insisted it was a matter of morals. She would not consort with someone who had been the madam, and maybe even a worker in Monsieur Habib's bordello. Even when slumming, my mother always valued managers more than workers. For once, I didn't care what my mother thought. I was very fond of Yvonne. She was always nice to me and once even took me to visit Lebanese friends who were studying at the University of Paris. The latter made me suspect she came from a far better background than my mother gave her credit for.

Most of the rooms in the hotel were rented by the hour. Some had permanent tenants, ladies of the evening who brought their customers there. I am determined to not use the word prostitute because it has such a pejorative meaning in our culture and doesn't do justice to these marvelous women. They had the hearts of gold ascribed to members of their profession and were the best and kindest neighbors I ever had. My favorite was Raymonde, a short, stringy brunette country girl from Normandy. She was in her forties, and no great beauty, but had a loyal following of steady customers who, like me, appreciated her unfailing kindness and good humor. However, these qualities weren't always enough for her pimp, a nasty little piece of work, who beat her when he had too much to drink. Every couple of weeks, we would hear his drunken curses and her screams begging him to stop. The next day I would see her go down the stairs, sporting a black eye or bruises on her face. She would smile at me, say hello, and act as if nothing had happened. As a little boy, I couldn't understand why she put up with him, why she didn't leave, and why no one stopped him or at least called the police. The sad reality in that subculture was that no one came between a macquereau (pimp) and his woman. To do so would beg for a slashing with the straight razor, which, according to local lore, every Algerian carried in their socks. Short of murder, everyone in this demimonde avoided the police at all costs. The other girls felt sorry for Raymonde only because her macquereau beat her more often than theirs.

We lived on the third floor. Dark stairs led to a long dark corridor carpeted with what had once been a thick red rug but was now threadbare, spotted, and musty. The hotel's transient clientele never complained about the poor lighting. Darkness suited their desire for anonymity, but those of us who had to live there found it oppressive;

it made the place feel even dingier than it was. We were lucky that our room, at least, was bright during the day. It had a window that faced the street.

Our room was fair sized, by our undemanding standards, around thirteen by fifteen feet. A two-burner stove with no oven, and a sink that dispensed only cold water, were in a shallow alcove in the back of the room. The bed and a rickety armoire filled most of the wall opposite the door. Four chairs and a wooden table covered by a cracked, yellowish green oilcloth pockmarked with cigarette burns occupied the center of the room. The quintessential appliance, one might even say the coat of arms of the profession practiced by most of the tenants, the bidet, lived between the bed and the sink.

At first, I shared the bed with my parents, but I wound up sleeping on a small, foldable wood and canvas cot we stored under the bed during the day and dragged out at night. As cramped as these lodgings might seem now viewed from an American perspective, the room felt spacious, and gave us the privacy we lacked in the Czechoslovakian displaced persons camp.

We ate breakfast and lunch at home and dinner at the free soup kitchen, set up by HIAS, on the Rue des Rosiers (the street of rose bushes). Rue des Rosiers had as few rose bushes as the Rue du Vertbois had green trees. It was a narrow winding street, only a few blocks long, in the Marais, the old Jewish section of Paris. Nicknamed the "Pletzle," meaning the small place or village square, it was the center of Jewish immigrant activity. Parisians claim that, if you sit long enough at the Café de la Paix in the Place de l'Opera, you will see everyone in the world pass by. On a less grandiose scale, if you hung out long enough on the "Pletzle" you would meet every Jewish immigrant in Paris. The Rue des Rosiers housed most of the aid organizations, a few kosher restaurants, some cheap clothing stores, and a flourishing black market specializing in gold, diamonds, and foreign currencies. It became my mom's base of operation.

After a few weeks in Paris my parents, who'd been storekeepers before the war, enrolled in trade schools set up by ORT (the Organization for Rehabilitation through Training), an aid organization which trained Jewish refugees in a variety of manual skills. This was emotionally very difficult for my parents. Being poor and taking charity, they believed, was only a temporary situation, but becoming manual workers showed them how low they'd sunk. Working with your hands placed you near the bottom of the Eastern European Jewish social scale. Working at a trade meant you were poor and doomed to remain so. It implied you were uneducated and lacked culture. In the strange world of the shtetl (small Jewish town), it was O.K. to be a poor scholar or a well-off storekeeper, but not a poor ignorant worker. "What can you expect of him?" My parents would sniffle, "He's a shoemaker!" To their credit, my parents swallowed their pride and tried to put the best face on things. It was then my mother first gave me her oft-repeated lecture on the inherent worth of honest labor, "You should never be ashamed of any work, even shoveling shit. As long as it's honest, and if it's what it takes to feed your family." I think I bought into the message far better than she did, especially the part about the work having to be honest, but I didn't grow up in a shtetl, and the different but just as bizarre set of values that drive me can't withstand scrutiny either.

My mother trained to be a finisher of men's suits – she sewed on buttons, labels, and finished buttonholes – while my dad learned how to make ladies' handbags. After six weeks of training, ORT found them jobs and the subsidies from HIAS were now supposed to stop. The aid organization expected us now to pay our rent and buy our own food and clothing. The "unfairness" of this set of arbitrary rules outraged my mom. HIAS had to help poor refugee Jews, and she would make sure they lived up to their obligation instead of hiding behind bureaucratic technicalities such as my parents now being employed. With me in tow looking waifish, she marched herself off to the HIAS offices after work. There she found, God knows how, the only benefit dispenser who was unattractive, unmarried, and unyoung. She poured out her tale of woe to this charming man, who she could see by his sympathetic face had a good heart and could understand the plight of a helpless widow and her poor sickly child, trying to survive in this strange and dangerous city. I was squirming with embarrassment. I never learned to feel comfortable with her blatant lying and was sure the poor man could see through her as clearly as I did, but he hadn't witnessed her act before, and I couldn't have been more wrong.

Like all virtuoso performers, once my mom got on a roll, the story, no matter how far removed from the truth, became her reality. She was inconsolable, cried, and shed genuine tears. She felt the pain, fear, and sense of hopelessness of a weak, scared, and lonely widow. The poor man was putty in her hands. Not only did he believe her story, but he fell head over heels with the beautiful young 'widow.' I am sure he saw himself as the brave knight-errant who would rescue her and, in return, win her heart and her hand. Not only did my mother continue to receive benefits for many months, but he swamped us with extra relief packages of food and clothing.

12

An Orphan No More

My parents worked all day, and I couldn't go to school since I didn't speak any French, so, once again, I wound up in a Jewish orphanage on the outskirts of Paris. This one fell somewhere between Zatrzebie, which deserved three Little Orphan Annies from the Michelin Guide to Orphanages, and Lodz, which rated a marginal one and a half. This orphanage occupied a large old mansion with modest grounds. The building was in a constant state of reconstruction, trying to convert spacious formal rooms into dormitories for a hundred boys and girls. Like Zatrzebie, and unlike Lodz, there were no definite plans for the orphans. It was a holding place until some unknown powers figured out what to do with us. By now I was an old pro at the orphanage game, and had no trouble adjusting to the new surroundings, which were far more comfortable and attractive than the hotel Francia. Still, given a choice, I would have preferred to remain with my parents. I missed them, but nobody asked my opinion, so the matter was out of my hands and I settled down in my latest home away from "home."

Unlike Zatrzebie, there was no established hierarchy among the inmates. We had a bimodal age distribution, a dozen big older kids who hung out together and bullied the rest of us when they deigned to notice we existed. I got more than my share of unwelcome attention because of my special status as a pretend orphan. I didn't understand their resentment; from where I stood, I didn't see any advantages to having parents. I didn't see them; they never came to visit. I didn't get presents or special treatment; if anything, I felt worse off. Their parents didn't choose to put them in an orphanage, they were dead and therefore unable to keep them; mine had a choice and they dumped me here because I was a burden, or even worse, because they didn't want me around. It may not have been true, but I felt abandoned.

I became ever more resentful of the bullying, until one day I lost it. I was playing with some other small boys on a mound of debris from the ongoing construction when one of the "elders," Armand, threw me off just for the hell of it. The act itself was unimportant, but it triggered all the rage building inside of me. To quote the insane anchorman in Network, "I was mad as hell, and I would not take it anymore." I grabbed a discarded two by four with rusty nails sticking out of it and, with all my strength, whacked Armand. Then I positioned myself on the mound, ready to hit him again if he came near me.

Shocked more by my impertinence than his own pain, Armand was determined to make me pay for my anarchistic act. He circled the mound a few times and tried to rush me, but each time he had to retreat as I swung the board full of nails, determined to inflict damage. Seeing no safe way to get at me, he pretended not to care and sauntered off with a few epithets thrown over his shoulder. The other boys and I knew better. I had faced the bully and won. To this day, even though I lay claim to being easygoing, I hate bullies, stand my ground, won't give an inch, and often lash out, no matter the cost. I want them to know they can't push me around.

Had I been of sound mind at that point, I would have declared victory and descended from the "mountain" to accept the adulation of my peers, but I was too far gone. I wanted everyone to know I'd had it, and no one would ever push me around or tell me what to do. So, I stayed on the mound and refused to get off, even when staff members told me to come to dinner. I was hungry and tired but determined. Around ten pm, I finally dropped my weapon, came off the mound and went to bed, hungry and a little embarrassed. The red veil of rage gone, and back in control of my faculties, I knew I had gone too far. Armand never tried to avenge himself, and no one ever bullied me again. I wanted to believe it was because everyone admired my courage, but it was more likely they thought I was crazy and didn't want to mess with a head case. That was my parents' interpretation of the incident when they heard about it from the counselors. From then on till the day they died, whenever I did something they disapproved of and I refused to see the error of my ways, they would chant in unison, "Armand wants me to come off the mound, so I won't do it."

For a few months, my life followed a predictable routine. The orphanage had two schools. We spent mornings learning French, and afternoons we studied the Torah. I loved the French classes, but balked at studying the Torah, which I found boring and uninspired. The curriculum and the pedagogical methods, though I didn't know it then, were the same as those inflicted on my father during his unhappy years at the Yeshiva. I wasn't interested in memorizing pieces of the Torah, or the disputations by revered sages on their meaning, and found many of the Old Testament stories hard to swallow. My teacher was furious, appalled I dared to question the immutable truths of the Torah, and when even a whipping didn't help, threw me out of the class, afraid my heresy might contaminate his other students. I refused to apologize or recant what I thought were legitimate questions, so the administrator of the orphanage assigned me to spend my afternoons sitting alone in the dormitory. That was fine with me. I spent the time reading books, unaware that my career as an orphan was about to end.

One day I started shivering at lunch and, when I went to the infirmary, they found out I was running a high fever. The nurse assumed I had the flu and applied the usual medieval medical treatments. She painted my mouth and throat with a black malodorous liquid, covered my front and back with "bagnkes," and forced me to drink gallons of hot tea while smothered under a down quilt. For those of you who are unfamiliar with eastern European peasant medicine, "bagnkes" are heavy wide mouth glass ampoules the size of a small peach. The person performing the procedure inserts a match or a lit stick into the ampoule, the air inside the bagnke becomes hot, and the "healer" presses the bagnke into the patient's flesh. As the air inside cools, it contracts and creates a vacuum that sucks the flesh into the ampoule; the suction, according to the most up to date medieval medical practice, draws the foul humors out of the body and restores health. After twenty minutes, the person applying the treatment breaks the vacuum and removes the ampoules. The treatment is painful and leaves behind forty or fifty silver dollar size hickeys. Despite the nurse's tender though useless ministrations, my temperature kept rising, and I began hallucinating. This scared the staff, and they called a doctor, who diagnosed my sickness as typhoid fever. An ambulance rushed me to the Pasteur Institute, where I remained for almost a month.

The doctors at the hospital had a tough time controlling my temperature, and I spent the first few days covered with ice packs. I was unconscious most of the time and hallucinated in glorious Technicolor and three-dimensional surround sound. I had lengthy discussions with kids I'd known in the orphanages, or odd people I'd met in the past, but most of the time I watched what I "knew" were mad Napoleonic war veterans marching back and forth in a disorderly military formation. They screamed while they marched, and I knew they were protesting something, but I couldn't understand a word of their complaints.

The temperature broke after a couple of weeks, and I became conscious of my surroundings. I was alone in a small but immaculate bright room. The accommodations were far better than anything I'd had in a long time. I was alone the entire day except for the occasional nurse who came to change my IV, check my temperature, or clean me up. The cleaning which occurred every morning around six am became a waking nightmare. An energetic and demented nurse with a fixation on clean privates. roused me from pleasant dreams by merciless, rough, and painful scrubbing of my nether parts.

"People are so ignorant," she growled. Her right hand swathed in what felt like a Brillo pad tried to rub off the skin from my most sensitive parts, while her left crushed my small, but much prized by me at least, "manhood."

"They think they wash their hands and face, and that makes them clean. A clean face means nothing! It's just a front. It's bullshit! What's important is to have a clean anus, a clean penis, and clean testicles. You must wash them every day as if your life depended on it. Every single day! Do you hear what I am telling you? Every single mother-loving day of your life!"

"Yes, Madame." I would gasp, unable to breathe through the pain.

"What will you do every day of your life after you leave the hospital?"

"Wash my anus, my penis, and my testicles every day, Madame!" I swore with the newfound fervor of a repentant heretic who'd found enlightenment after extensive religious instruction on the rack.

"No, you won't! You men are all the same, a bunch of lying bastards! You just say it to shut me up. Well, I don't care! It's your funeral! Go ahead! Go through life carrying germs in your stinking asshole!" She accompanied this last verbal parting shot by flinging away my, by then, shriveled and aching, offending parts.

The rest of the nurses were far saner and much nicer. I didn't get any solid food for the first two weeks, and once I started feeling better, I was ready to eat the proverbial horse. The nurses, aware of my ravenous appetite, fed me double meals and sneaked extra goodies throughout the day. My parents came to see me often, even though the hospital was a long way from the hotel. In some ways, I started thinking being sick wasn't such a terrible deal. I had my room, and nobody, except for my morning nurse Florence Frightingale, bullied me. All the other nurses were stuffing me with food and kindness, and best of all, I got to see my parents almost every day. I could live with that. The sickness had an unexpected but much appreciated side benefit: it convinced my parents they couldn't trust an orphanage to take good care of me, so when I left the hospital, I returned with them to the hotel Francia.

13

Return to "Normal"

My parents' fortunes improved during my stay in the orphanage. Mom quit her job at the factory and was once more wheeling and dealing in the black market and involved in other extra-legal activities. She convinced Mr. Habib she would keep his hotel fully rented if he gave her the right to pick the prospective tenants. She used this power to sell the rooms to other refugees looking for a cheap place to live. As a side benefit, she recruited a few of them as workers in the handbag manufacturing contract business my parents established in our hotel room. My dad, while a difficult human being, was, contrary to my mom's impassioned put downs, very intelligent and competent; it took him only two or three months to learn all he needed to know about making bags. Once he was sure he knew what he was doing, he contracted with manufacturers to make bags for them at a fixed cost if they provided the raw materials and patterns.

My parents bought two old sewing machines and squeezed them into the room by placing them at right angles to each other under the window. The dining room table became the cutting board and my mother recruited four refugees who needed a job, any job, and who agreed to work for meager wages. All four had been professionals before the war and all had high hopes for a better future, but in the meantime, they had to eat. The two sewing machine operators were brothers who'd been rabbinical students before the war. The fellow who put the clutches on bags was a dentist, and the cutter was a naturopath, a follower of Dr. Coué. Coué was a 1920s proponent of positive thinking who encouraged people to start each morning by saying out loud, "Every day in every way I am getting better and better." The other workers laughed at him but were a little awed by his demonstrations of the power of positive thinking. He would stand with his arms extended and challenge the others to pull his arms down. All three pulled and even hung on his arms but couldn't budge them. No one understood how he did it, so the obvious conclusion was he was weird. His bizarre ideas about food reinforced their opinion. Among his many dietary heresies were the "insane" beliefs that fat and refined sugar were bad for you, and that most of the nutrients in fruits were in the skin. He ate oranges, peels and all. My parents and the other workers made fun of him, but he never reacted to their scoffing. He was a very sweet man and a hell of a cutter.

During the day, our room was so crowded there was no room to move; the cutter and the framer had to work in shifts since they both used the table. The cutter worked from eight am to two pm, and then the framer would take over till seven or eight in the evening. At night after dinner, most often thick soup and bread, many of the new hotel residents, refugees who'd bought rooms in the hotel from my mother, would gather in our room for endless glasses of tea and conversation.

While the adults argued and slurped tea, I crawled under the table with a book, where I created a private space; years in the cellar made me an expert on creating an environment where I shut out all distractions. Sometimes, when I had nothing left to read, I would listen in. The discussions were always about what was the best place to emigrate. No one wanted to stay in Europe; after the war, no one felt safe there. They all wanted to get as far away as possible from the site of the Holocaust. Everyone wanted to go to America, but the Polish quota was tiny, and one had to wait many years with no guarantee of ever getting there. Palestine was the second choice of many, but the British, "Filthy anti-Semites, may God give them boils in the most painful places," were blockading the Promised Land, and sent Jews, caught trying to sneak in, to holding camps in Cyprus. It was easier to get a visa to Canada, Australia, South Africa, and most of the South American countries, but no one knew anything about these places. What were they like? Did they have Jews? Could one make a living there? What was one to do? Play the long shot and wait for a visa to America or take the surer but scarier path and emigrate to these unknown countries?

The other topic on everyone's mind was missing spouses. We were one of the few intact families; most refugees became separated from their spouses and children during the war. It was a fair assumption the children were dead; few survived the Nazi killing machine, especially when separated from their parents. However, one's husband or wife might still be alive, even if their name didn't appear on any of the survivor lists put together by nongovernmental aid organizations. It was a chaotic time. People floated from one country or one displaced people's camp to another, and everyone knew the lists were less than definitive. These solid middle-class people, who had followed a strict social and moral code before the war, felt trapped on the horns of a painful dilemma. The concept of living together outside of marriage was unthinkable before the war, and everyone ostracized people engaged in such shameless behavior. But human beings are social creatures, and after years of focusing only on survival, they craved intimacy and companionship. They coupled up with new partners and lived with them in a state of suspended animation. Each knew a missing spouse might reappear, which would end their relationship, or at least cause an enormous amount of angst. The cataclysm they'd lived through suspended so many of the rules that regulated their lives before the war, and no one thought of questioning this previously unacceptable behavior.

My favorites among these guests were Mr. Yanofsky, who remained a family friend till his death many years later in the United States, and Ruchl Rellis, a Romanian soprano and her Gentile "husband." Before the war, Mr. Yanofsky was a journalist for a Yiddish newspaper in Warsaw. He became separated from his wife and children while they were trying to escape to Russia ahead of the advancing German armies. He left them near the border while he went looking for a place to stay on the Russian side. The Russians closed the frontier, and he could not get back to his family. They died in a German concentration camp, and the Russians sent him to a slave labor camp in Siberia. Life in the Gulag was hard for an intellectual who'd never experienced such harsh climatic conditions, or hard physical labor. He survived but came out of Siberia crippled with a twisted back. However, the physical pain he endured for the rest of his life was nothing compared to the emotional pain and guilt he felt whenever he thought about what he could or should have done to save his wife and children. Despite suffering from this trauma, he remained a wonderful, kind, and gentle person. I never heard him complain or feel sorry for himself; he was always ready to help others. Even my dad, who was leery of everyone, respected and trusted him.

Ruchl Rellis was a horse of a different color; a dark-haired, handsome woman of a certain age, blessed with a large singing voice and figure to match. No one knew much about her, or her "husband-manager's" past. We called him Ignysty Pyfteh, because of his constant use of that expression as a noun, verb, adjective, or adverb in a broad range of contexts. We never understood its meaning, and he never volunteered an explanation. It just became both his trademark and his nickname. Ruchl could not get work as a singer, and since her French was poor, her only choice was the Yiddish theater. Thanks to her, we got free tickets and became regular attendees.

I loved the Yiddish theater, even though all the plays, just like romance novels, followed a well-known but beloved formula. In the first act, a good-looking scoundrel, or even worse, a gentile, seduces an innocent young woman. She refuses to listen to her parents' wise and tearful entreaties and runs off with the miscreant. In the second act, the broken-hearted parents try to rebuild their lives and forget the wretched girl but they can't, of course. They are Jewish parents with hearts as big as the Russian Steppes, and you cry as you watch them suffer, bemoaning the fate of their lost child. The third act brings the obvious denouement; the wretched girl is now the mother of a small child or at least pregnant, abandoned by the scoundrel her parents warned her against. She is penniless with no place to go, and realizes how wrong she was not to have heeded her parents' warnings. She comes home a sadder but wiser woman. Her magnanimous parents forgive her and take her and the baby in. Her life, thanks to her foolishness, is now over, but there is a baby to bring up, and a debt of gratitude and repentance she owes her parents for their generosity and forgiveness. The curtain comes down on an audience bathed in satisfying tears.

La Rellis was too mature to play the foolish maiden, and not good enough to play the star tragic role of the wise and loving mother. The director relegated her to the comic relief role of the virago next door, who elicits laughs by bullying and pushing her puny husband around the stage. She took to the role with such zeal her stage husband's real-life wife begged her to restrain her acting fervor and spare his life. The poor man had a heart condition and came home bruised after each performance.

My father didn't need my mother's help to run the contracting operation, and she was free to devote her full attention to her extra-legal activities. She hooked up with a local Jewish jeweler named

Frydman and developed a fair-sized watch smuggling operation from Switzerland. Every couple of weeks, she took a train to Geneva or Zurich with empty valises and a handbag full of dollars. She returned the next day with an empty handbag and valises full of brand name watches like Omega, Movado, Patek, and Schaffhausen. I was never sure whether she bought the watches from a legitimate wholesaler and made a profit by avoiding the hefty import tariff, or whether she bought them from someone expert at catching goods falling off a truck.

My mom preferred not to know the provenance of her purchases, which allowed her conscience to remain pristine. In her mind, her part of the transaction was always beyond reproach; she paid honest dollars for desirable goods and sold them at what she considered a fair price, meaning the most she could get. If the people who sold her the watches stole them, the sin belonged to the thief, not her. It never occurred to her that smuggling might be wrong. It was a profitable business open to the few gutsy and clever people, like herself, who knew how to charm, and if necessary, bribe the right customs people. Her worldview and ethical code became set during the war. There was no difference between smuggling watches into France and smuggling wheat into the ghetto. Lying to aid agencies to get extra benefits was the same as telling Mrs. Zaremba she would share in our fictitious fortune in return for funding our survival. My mom drew the line at stealing and murder or harming someone, but the powers that be had broken their social contract with her, and she felt free to operate guided only by what she knew helped her survive or prosper.

When my mom wasn't smuggling watches, one could always find her on the Rue des Rosiers (the Pletzle) where she indulged in her favorite profession, black marketing in foreign currency. When I wasn't in school, I would often accompany her, reprising my old role of "mule," an unobvious carrier of sizable sums of illegal currency. Aside from the pain of having my cheeks and the underside of my chin tweaked by iron-gripped old men, I rather enjoyed the experience. It was an exotic and exciting bazaar, where millions of dollars changed hands every minute, and a man's word was his bond. There were no written agreements, but no one ever reneged because if he did, the word would spread, and he would be out of business. My mom was the only woman trader, as far as I know, and I was the only child around. Many of the dealers went out of their way to teach me the tricks of the trade or just to amuse me. I learned how to count money fast, just like a banker, and how to spot a fake diamond; a drop of water beads up on a diamond, but spreads on glass or cubic zirconia. The latter, I realized many years later when I studied surface chemistry, was sound science and involved differences in the surface energies of diamond and glass. Another trick, also based on good science, involved the cracking of an egg. Eggs are very fragile when squeezed around the equator but will not break even under great pressure when you apply pressure at the poles.

My mother did very well on the black market, but her most profitable day resulted from a potential disaster, a chaotic situation that always brought out the "best" in her. The Paris police knew all about the black market on the Pletzl but ignored it most of the time, just like they ignored prostitution, which became illegal only because of the "unfortunate" intrusion into French life and culture by a "frustrated" American busybody named Martha Richard. However, as with prostitution, every once in a while, the police felt pressure to show they were enforcing the laws of the land. Every few months, they blockaded the exits out of the Rue des Rosiers with police vans, arrested everyone, and confiscated the illegal contraband. The colloquial name for these vans was paniers a salade, (salad baskets) because during sweeps, those arrested were unceremoniously tossed into them like handfuls of lettuce. My mother was in the Pletzle during one of these raids, and while everyone else panicked and ran every which way, she alone kept her wits. She stopped several distraught dealers and guaranteed she would get their money out for a ten percent commission. It was a no-lose proposition for them. They would lose everything if caught by the police and a ten percent commission was a bargain if, by some miracle, my mother got their money out. They filled up the two big empty bags she'd brought to shop for groceries on her way home. Weighed down by the two heavy bags filled with foreign currencies, she stumbled towards the advancing police, while everyone else was running away in the opposite direction.

"Excuse me, gentlemen," she asked, wiping the sweat from her forehead, in as poor French as she could muster but the policemen could still understand, "I am looking for pyfteh rue Ignisty (I hope you recognize the origin of this address), I have been walking around in circles for hours. I am from out of town, and I promised my friend back home to deliver these bags to her daughter who lives at number pyfteh rue Ignisty." The policemen looked in vain for rue Ignisty in the little black guidebooks they all carried but were desolated (the French are never just sorry) as they could find no trace of rue Ignisty or even anything close.

"Well, I don't know how, but I must have gotten it wrong," she said. "I'll just have to call my friend, get the right address when I get back to the hotel, and return later. I am worn out from all this wandering around in vain. Would one of you kind gentlemen please get me a taxi so I can go back to the hotel and lie down? I don't think I have the strength to walk back."

No policeman could imagine anyone carrying a fortune in black market money would have the chutzpah to approach them instead of running away, so they got her a taxi and apologized again for their inability to help her locate rue Ignisty. My mother was ecstatic for days. She was always in an excellent mood after a clever coup. The amount of money she made was far less important than demonstrating once again that she was smarter, more competent, and had bigger balls than anyone else. The money was just a way of keeping score; what mattered was the artistry of the performance. Had it been a bullfight, she would have given herself the tail and both ears for her coup that day.

While my dad ran the handbag contracting business, and my mom bent the laws of various countries, I started formal schooling at the local elementary school a few blocks from the hotel Francia. For the first time, I was in school, surrounded by kids who weren't interested in either bullying or beating me up. It was a blast. I made a lot of friends, especially Albert Rubman, a native Parisian Jew whose parents owned a small clothing shop, and Guy de Passoz, who lived across the street from the hotel. Neighborhood gossips claimed Guy was the love child of a French working-class girl and a Portuguese nobleman who, lacking both character and originality, abandoned her when she became pregnant. Guy was not only smart (we always battled for first place on exams), he was one of those fortunate people who effortlessly exuded cool. Everyone ascribed his natural elegance and unstudied nonchalant air to the noble, if faithless, blood coursing through his veins. We were living under the Third Republic, but at heart every self-respecting Frenchman is a closet monarchist.

I loved going to school. For the first time in my life, I was getting validation. I found out I had a good mind and had no trouble absorbing whatever knowledge the teachers threw at me. In the French school system, students are ranked based on their grades, and it was great, for a change, to be first, or at worst second on days when Guy beat me out. Best of all, the working-class neighborhood kids didn't care I was Jewish, or resent me for not being an orphan. They accepted or rejected me on my own merits. It was nice to find out that based on these criteria, I was fine.

School became a haven for me; the classroom was so much more spacious and peaceful than our crowded, noisy, and hysterical one-room home/factory. My mom, who went off for hours at a time every other day or so on passionate, full-throated riffs detailing my father's meanness, cruelty, and incompetence, provided the hysteria. She contrasted my father's failings and character flaws with a detailed list of her matchless qualities -- her kindheartedness, her generosity, her matchless housekeeping and business skills. This recital of his sins and her virtues led to heartbreaking and tearful bemoaning of her undeserved plight. The Ruler of the Universe knew how she suffered; even more than the Israelites ever did in Egypt. He took pity on their misery and set them free. When, oh, when would he do the same for her? My father never replied. He stayed silent in his chair, his hands in his pockets, his head buried between his raised shoulders, his upper teeth biting down on his lower lip as if to lock in whatever inappropriate words might escape from his mouth.

These passion plays always ended in the same dramatic fashion; my mother, inflamed by her own rhetorical flights, could not restrain herself any longer. She threw herself at my father and tried to scratch his miserable face. He'd grab her wrists in self-defense, and after a few seconds of struggle during which she let the rest of the hotel know she was being abused, she collapsed to the floor and fainted.

My father would fall on his knees next to her prostrate body, kiss her limp hands, beg her forgiveness, and pray for her to come back to life. After a while, to his great joy, her eyes would open, she would get up as if nothing happened, and normalcy or what passed for it in our lives returned to our cramped little quarters.

I hated these scenes; I was furious with my mom for her self-indulgent eruptions, but knew they meant nothing. She just needed to vent and once she got on a roll, she couldn't stop; her grievances became more real than reality and the drama just had to play itself out. I was much angrier with my dad for not being a "man" and standing up to her. I couldn't believe he didn't see through her act and at least call her bluff by ignoring her phony fainting scenes.

One night I took matters into my own hands, and when she "fainted" I threw a pot of cold water on her face to prove she was faking. She came to, sputtering with rage, and I got a thorough beating from both parents united in outrage at my wanton act of filial disrespect. I learned an important lesson that night: never become the third actor in a tightly scripted two-character play.

Given a choice between going home and staying in school, I always chose the latter. School ended at four, but children whose parents worked late could stay till six. I registered for the program and told my parents it was mandatory. Watching my mother all these years, I learned sometimes one needs to mold the truth to achieve desired outcomes. The school expected we would use those two hours to do our homework, but the study room had no lights and during winter by five o'clock it was too dark to do anything, so the monitor read to us by candlelight. Jack London's White Fang was our favorite. We sat in the dark, huddled together to keep warm in the unheated room, and listened entranced to his disembodied voice describe a pack of wolves stalking a lone man in the Yukon. We felt the man's fear, the desperate loneliness of the white winter wasteland, the strength-sapping cold, but we persevered and willed him to survive against all odds. The six o'clock bell would break the spell and we wandered home, consoled only by the knowledge we would be back in magic land the next evening. Sometimes I wouldn't go home even then. I wandered the streets until I became too tired or too hungry. My parents were so wrapped up in their own personal and common struggles they never noticed when I came home as long as I was there for dinner, sometimes between eight and nine.

At the end of the year, we all took the age eleven entrance exam for the College Turgot, our local Lycée. Those who passed continued their academic careers; the rest remained in elementary school for another three years until they turned fourteen, when they became apprenticed at some trade, or just went to work. It may seem harsh to have your future decided at such an early age, but the French, and most Europeans, view education beyond the point of functional literacy as a privilege reserved for the intellectually endowed. It is an elitist position, but its flaws, while different, are no worse than the American custom of warehousing students in schools where they linger for years with very little knowledge or skills to show for all the time and money spent on this exercise in "democracy." The French system has a lifesaving option for first-time losers; they get a second and final chance the next year. I was twelve when I took it, so for me, this was it. There was no tomorrow; However, I didn't understand the seriousness of the situation and felt no pressure.

Albert, Guy, and I were the only three from our school to pass, and since we all scored in the top five percent, we wound up in an experimental class taught along the precepts of Jean Jacques Rousseau. We had the best teachers in the school who emphasized learning rather than memorization. They eschewed rigid lectures and the traditional strict discipline, encouraged lively debate and, for a French school, tolerated a rather scandalous lack of order and decorum. The only fly in my ointment was shop, a heretical concept for a Lycée supposed to turn out future intellectuals, not laborers. Old Jean Jacques believed in a concept that, I'm sure, he never practiced himself: that everyone should know how to work with their hands. So twice a week, I maimed mine in vain attempts at carpentry and metalwork. My scarred hands were an insignificant price to pay for what was, overall, an exhilarating experience.

Looking back at the rest of my overlong academic career, I realized I never enjoyed learning as much as I did that year. In other settings, I became good at playing the academic game and passing tests, but it was joyless work I performed doggedly, because I saw it as my only ticket out of the ghetto. My use of that last term may surprise you, but ghetto is as much a psychological as a physical prison. I've lived in two of the greatest, most cosmopolitan cities in the world, Paris and New York, but my environment, composed of working-class and small business-owning Jews, limited my world view. Their values, traditions, and resentments brought over from the shtetl defined the boundaries.

You could see "them" on the other side of the invisible wall, but you never crossed the line. These boundaries defined what was conceivable: your life, your aspirations, your choices. It wasn't much.

At Turgot, Guy and I continued our fierce, though friendly, rivalry for academic leadership. He came in first to my second in math and science while I won in French, Latin, English and history. We would alternate taking first place in geography, and he would bury me in art, music, gym, and, as mentioned, my personal Waterloo, shop. I spent most of my free time with Albert. We wandered around town, visited museums, or saw the occasional movie, but we spent most of our time hanging around his house. He lived in a two-bedroom apartment with his parents and an older brother. I thought this was the height of extravagant luxury until I visited another classmate, Lionel Chouchan. I knew Chouchan's family had money. They owned an enormous furniture store, the "Meuble d'Or" on the Boulevard Sebastopol, but I never realized how much money they had until I saw how they lived.

One day Chouchan (we weren't close enough to call each other by our first names) asked me to go play at his house after school and, since I liked him, I agreed. He lived five blocks from the Hotel Francia, right off the Boulevard Sebastopol, but the economic and social distance between our worlds had galactic dimensions. His family lived in one of those grand old sandstone buildings that grace Parisian boulevards. They occupied an entire floor, five bedrooms, a grand salon, a dining room, a library, and servant quarters. The air smelled of floor polish instead of cabbage and machine oil. Fine rugs instead of torn linoleum covered their floors, and imposing pieces of expensive furniture filled each room.

Chouchan led me to his bedroom. Holy shit! His own room! It was bigger than our place at the Hotel Francia and furnished in classic Young Master. Books and games filled the shelves along the wall; we picked one that was an early board version of Where is Carmen San Diego. I'd never owned or seen a board game. It was so much fun; I thought I had died and gone to heaven, but I was only in its antechamber. Heaven came next. Albert asked me if I wanted some Grenadine. I didn't know what it was but, too embarrassed to admit it, said sure. Chouchan rang a little bell and instructed the "genie" Robert, a wizened little man in formal attire who materialized on the third ring, to provide us with two Grenadines and cookies. I had tasted nothing so delicious before, and for the first time in my life, became aware we were poor. I liked Chouchan, but we never became close. The gulf between our worlds was just too large, and I preferred not to face the reality of our families' relative positions in life. As long as I hung around with the rest of the proletariat, I could think of myself as middle class. After all, in my normal world, we were at least as good as the "Ladies" and better than their sleazy macquereaux.

My parents' contracting business prospered. My father taught himself how to design handbags, and my parents moved up the food chain, opening their own factory specializing in plastic and synthetic suede knockoffs of expensive bags sold in the fancy stores on the Grand Boulevards or the Champs Elysée. The operation became too big for the hotel room and my parents bought a furnished apartment in an old, grimy building at 5 rue de Tracy, a dark, narrow street off the Boulevard Sebastopol. I was thrilled; this was our first proper home since before the war. It was a fourth-floor walkup. A small foyer led to a narrow galley kitchen through one door, and two fair sized rooms through another; these two became the factory. The living room, where I slept like a prince on my very own studio bed that converted into a couch during the day, was behind those two rooms and led to my parents' bedroom in the back. We still had to use a two-stepper bathroom in the hall, but we shared it with only one other family.

There was no bathtub or shower, although for the first time in our lives we had running hot water in the kitchen sink. We continued our habit of going to the public baths on Sunday mornings. The baths were like a cafe; one met the entire neighborhood and caught up on the week's gossip while waiting your turn. You got 40 minutes for a bath and 20 minutes for a shower. Some rooms had two or three bathtubs for the communal cleansing of entire families. I found out later the ladies, who cleaned the bathtubs, would also help soap you up or get you off for a nominal fee. Now that's what I call full service.

As our economic position continued improving, my parents made Sunday not just the weekly bath day but also, for our family, a day of total sloth and debauchery. After the Sunday bath, we adjourned to a kosher restaurant on rue Notre Dame de Lorette. For those who grew up taking restaurants and takeout food for granted, this may not seem earthshaking. In our universe, spending 'exorbitant' sums of money for a meal my mother could cook way, way, way, way better, with higher quality fresh ingredients, and for only a few "pennies" was equivalent to throwing coins in a fountain, another stupid waste of money that reflected poorly not just on one's intelligence, but also on one's moral character. I didn't care what madness overcame my parents; I didn't dare entertain the heretical notion that the restaurant's chef cooked better than my mother, but I dreamt all week of these Sunday feasts. After the late lunch, we strolled down the grand boulevards up to the Place de l'Opera, where we drank a glass of beer at the Café de la Paix. Yes, Lord, the debauchery never stopped. We returned home late in the evening, exhausted but ecstatic; these were some of the happiest days of my life.

14

The Lycée Charlemagne

I loved being a student at the college Turgot, but my parents harbored higher hopes for my future. They wanted me to become a doctor. What Jewish parents don't dream of this for their son? They thought I would be better prepared for this exalted profession at one of the four elite Grand Lycées and transferred me to the Lycée Charlemagne. They had good intentions, but so is the pavement of the road to hell, and the result was disastrous. The Lycée Charlemagne was three or four miles from home, which was not the problem. I walked there and used the money my parents gave me for Metro tickets to buy books from the bouquiniers, booksellers on the banks of the river Seine. The problem was that because it was an elite institution, its student body came from the richest and most exclusive sections of Paris, far removed from the Hotel Francia, which was on the other, not-good side of the tracks. Going to the Lycée Charlemagne separated me from all my friends, and I missed the free atmosphere I had enjoyed so much at Turgot.

Charlemagne was the exact opposite of my previous school. It was an austere institution, run with an iron fist by a cadre of little despots with inflated opinions of their own importance. They were here to transmit knowledge, and since they, not the students, were its sole repository, questions or attempts at dialogue were a sign of impertinence, or at the very least, a shocking lack of self-control. The teachers were quick to inflict physical pain on any miscreant who dared to even chafe under the absolute authority granted to them by the ministry of education.

The students were even worse than the faculty. They all came from upper class Catholic families. I was the only Jew, and the only kid whose father wasn't a count, a duke, a banker, or at least an upper-level bureaucrat. They picked on me at first until they found out I would take them on when confronted with anti-Semitic taunts, even if they were bigger and stronger. It became obvious I refused to turn the other cheek. How unchristian of me. I lost most of the fights but inflicted enough pain to persuade them it was wiser to just shun me.

I was unhappy at the Lycée Charlemagne; I felt isolated and chafed under the tyrannical discipline of the faculty. I lost interest in my studies and escaped even more into books. Reading became my haven; I used books to escape my unhappy reality, just as I had used my imagination when we were hiding out in the cellar. Every Sunday, before we went to the public baths, I'd bring the previous week's batch of books back to the library, and stagger home under the load of next week's supply. I became friends with the librarians and after a while they let me roam through the stocks by myself, instead of having to ask for specific books. I discovered a lot of authors this way and gained a wonderful education in French literature during those years. There were very few books by foreign authors. This was a neighborhood library. It had only so much space and money and wasn't about to waste them on "inferior" writers. I had to wait to come to America to discover Shakespeare, Dickens, Goethe, Mann, Tolstoy, Dostoevsky, and other foreign, and therefore lesser, authors.

Being a typical teenager, I acted out my unhappiness by staging psychological guerilla warfare against my oppressors. I indulged in a variety of random subversive acts: greased the blackboards, put glue on their chairs, marbles under the legs of their desks, even a dead rat in the music teacher's handbag, the only woman and innocent party on the faculty. I wanted my teachers to be on edge and as frustrated as I felt in their classrooms. My reward was grudging admiration from my classmates, and regular beatings, with bare hands, rulers, wooden pointers, or even willow branches soaked in brine, by an outraged faculty. I spent most of my supposed free Thursdays in detention writing 5000 times, "I will never again show disrespect for my teacher and behave like an ignorant savage in class." Or something else just as instructive and uplifting. Only one teacher, Monsieur Allegret, who taught science and was the resident communist, bore me no ill will, and even saw in me a kindred spirit.

"I appreciate your desire to rebel, Fryd, it shows a laudable awareness of the inequities of the system, but not in my classroom, you little hoodlum!" He'd tell me while whacking me over the head with a meter stick. "You're going to detention this Thursday, mon vieux, where you will write a synopsis and your thoughts on Das Kapital that will show me you understand the need for revolutionary discipline. I'll give you a copy after class. Now get out of here and go annoy your fascist teachers."

Monsieur Allegret took me to a few Communist rallies at the Velodrome (the bicycle racing arena) and while I agreed with slogans such as, "From each according to his ability, to each according to his needs," I never became a convert. I found the meetings to be hokey, and the leadership as controlling as the system they opposed, but I loved the bike races used to attract bigger crowds.

I ignored the physical punishments from teachers, but detentions were a bigger problem. When you received a detention, you had to take a notice of your dishonorable behavior home on Tuesday, and return it signed by your parents on Thursday when you came to serve your sentence. My parents never questioned why I left home early on my days off instead of sleeping in. As long as I wasn't in the way, everything was fine. I learned to counterfeit my father's signature and for quite a while, all was well, even though I exceeded the detention quota necessary for expulsion. The Lycée's principal allowed me to remain in school despite my mounting pile of detention slips, only because I was the perennial winner of the Latin prize. A trophy as valued in Paris as a football championship is here.

This uncomfortable equilibrium could have gone on forever if, during my second year at Charlemagne, I hadn't fallen afoul of my personal nemesis, MONSIEUR EDOUARD THE LATIN AND FRENCH PROFESSOR. MONSIEUR EDOUARD, an antique bullfrog dressed in drab colored three-piece suits shiny with age, thought of himself in capital letters far bigger than I used on this page. He spent at least half of his classes sharing with us his exalted opinion of his importance. We heard cautionary tales about insolent publishers who incurred his wrath by ignoring his suggestions for improving their Latin grammar textbooks; he stopped using them, so the books were now out of print. There were also, from time to time, impudent administrators who dared to question his unimpeachable pedagogical methods; he put them in their place and forced them to suffer with inferior replacements when MONSIEUR EDOUARD left their pathetic institutions for Lycées blessed with more enlightened principals. What made it all worthwhile for him, however, was the occasional brilliant student who, thanks to MONSIEUR EDOUARD, learned to write a decent sentence. He subjected us to endless readings of these model essays that lived up to his exacting standards and deserved a stratospheric grade as high as an eighty. He expected us to strive for such perfection and, though MONSIEUR EDOUARD doubted it, he hoped one of us, following his guidance, might produce a paper worthy of boring future classes.

I was smart enough to know not to trifle with MONSIEUR EDOUARD, and behaved as well as I could in his class, but it was all to no avail. Maybe he was anti-Semitic, which I think he was, or maybe, like Monsieur Allegret, he recognized my rebellious streak, but unlike him, instead of a potential convert, he saw the enemy. My grades in his classes were barely passing. Even though every year I won the Latin prize, the best I could get from him was a C. My worst moments occurred at the end of each marking period. That was when the EDOUARD ORACLE announced to a trembling class of 13- and 14-year-olds, who of us would pass their Baccalaureate exams at eighteen and go on to a university, and who would fail and become a shopkeeper. You must pass this three-day examination after you graduate from the Lycée to be admitted to a University, and so, like the Lycée's entrance examination, it determined the rest of your life. When he came to me, he always stopped, stared down his nose, sniffed for emphasis, and rendered my academic death sentence. "Fryd? Possible, but very unlikely." Even though deep in my heart I saw him for what he was, a pathetic blowhard, I always felt crushed. What would I do if he were right? It is hard to have your dreams destroyed and discarded with the garbage before you're even sure what they are.

My Waterloo occurred during a French class. MONSIEUR EDOUARD had been waxing eloquent about his favorite topic, himself, for almost an hour. I had finished reading the library book I brought with me to ease the tedium and, in a moment of bored madness, committed an act so scandalous that later even I couldn't believe I was capable of such temerity, such an act of uncivil disobedience! I turned to one of the other students and passed the back of my hand, back and forth, over my cheek. This gesture, which has no meaning in the United States, is a French slang expression implying MONSIEUR EDOUARD bored me. The student for whom I intended the gesture didn't catch it, but the heinous act didn't escape MONSIEUR EDOUARD, who was always alert for any signs of impudence, meaning anything short of rapt and reverent attention. He gasped, and the breath intake was so violent his face turned dark crimson, and veins as thick as garden snakes fought their way through the fat to emerge, throbbing the length of his neck and forehead. For what seemed like eternity, he couldn't utter a word. When he recovered his composure, he drew himself up to his full Olympian height of five foot three or four, and with a voice still choked with repressed rage he passed my academic death sentence. He ordered me to proceed to the Principal's office. Once there, I was to transmit to him MONSIEUR EDOUARD's decision to have me expelled from the Lycée. I was clearly incapable of benefiting from a classical education and, therefore, needed to be excised like a malignant tumor before I contaminated the rest of the healthy student body. He banished me from the classroom with a final, vengeful, dismissive gesture. Adam cast out of Paradise couldn't have felt greater despair and regret, and he at least could lay part of the blame on Eve and the snake, while I was the sole architect of my downfall.

I'd never been so afraid; dismissal from one Lycée meant dismissal from all. Cast out of the French educational system, this was the end of my education. Doomed, I prayed for help from the God I wasn't sure I believed in anymore, with a fervor I haven't duplicated since. Maybe God listened to me, or maybe I was just lucky, but the Principal was busy with a visitor and couldn't see me. He was still busy when the class bell rang for recess, and I saw a slim opportunity for salvation. I raced back to the classroom, fell on my knees before MONSIEUR EDOUARD. Sobbing hysterically, I confessed all my sins, both those of thought and deed. I flagellated myself, promised him that should he deign to forgive me I would be a new and better man, well, at least a better boy. This self-abasement lasted through most of the class break while MONSIEUR EDOUARD stood still, looking down upon me with obvious contempt. My classmates, mesmerized by this mini-passion play, watched with rapt attention. When the class bell rang,

MONSIEUR EDOUARD turned his back to me and, without a word, waddled away ponderously towards the classroom. A strange calm descended upon me; certain I lost all, both hope and despair were removed. I was getting off my knees, ready to pay for my transgression in the principal's office, when the GREAT MAN stopped at the classroom door, turned, and waved me over.

"I am sure I'll regret my decision, but being who I am, I am always willing to give anyone another chance, no matter how undeserved and undeserving. In your case, it is unlikely that you have it in your essence to appreciate what I am doing for you, or to learn from it. Your depraved spirit will lead to your ultimate downfall. What it will be, alcohol, opium, or just general depravity, I don't know, but I am sure you will wind up in jail or in the gutter, but no one will say I didn't give you a chance to overcome your base nature."

I didn't care about my doomed future. All I knew was thanks to a miracle I got a reprieve, and could breathe again, at least for the time being. MONSIEUR EDOUARD commuted my sentence and gave me a chance to avoid the need to endure a lifetime of honest but hard physical labor.

However, one couldn't commit such a grievous act of lèse-majesté and escape unscathed. The Principal on MONSIEUR EDOUARD'S advice didn't expel me but insisted on meeting my parents. He wanted to find out why they hadn't exerted more effort, i.e. more punishment, to affect a change in my behavior. They had signed all the detention slips and announcements of suspension. They knew the enormity and persistence of my scholastic transgressions. Why hadn't they done more, and what did they plan to do now?

My parents didn't feel confident in their command of the French language, and they were busy running the business, so they sent one of their workers, Monsieur Gottesman, a native French Jew who had become our new framer. Monsieur Gottesman was a lovely man who ruined his life when he became a gambling addict. He had once been a successful handbag manufacturer himself but lost both his business and his family because of his inability to either stop betting on the ponies or learn how to handicap a race. My parents used him as a golden example of the doom that befell degenerates; degeneracy was a broad category covering all "excessive" indulgences, be they gambling, womanizing, drinking, or, just as deplorable, eating a whole pound of meat at one sitting.

Monsieur Gottesman sympathized with my plight, but he had to report to my parents what he heard from the Principal. My parents learned about a year and a half's worth of my sins, a rather impressive collection if I say so myself. As expected, they found my scandalous behavior appalling; it was so un-Jewish, feh! How could I bring such shame on the family? How could they face their friends? What would become of a hooligan like me? They had an obvious answer to that last question. A child who counterfeits his parents' signature at fourteen will, without doubt, wind up in jail for murder or at least armed robbery by the time he reaches adulthood. My future seemed set, and it looked bleak. All the authority figures in my life, both my parents, and MONSIEUR EDOUARD, agreed on a common prognosis: I was doomed, destined to become a jailbird when I grew up. Filled with remorse and fear, I prayed for divine intervention. Was there no hope for me? What could I do to get off this hideous road that led to a life of crime? I wasn't just afraid of winding up in jail; I didn't fancy either the lifestyle or the practice of the criminal profession.

There was no point in begging for mercy when my parents tried to beat the evil out of my sinful body over the next few weeks. I understood, even shared, their disappointment, and agreed with their assessment of the magnitude of my guilt. The punishment that stung most was having to sit there while my parents shared with everyone they knew the sad tale of my depraved behavior. My head bowed; I covered my eyes in the vain hope that not seeing them made me invisible. Even though I knew it wasn't true, it made the experience a little more bearable, and I wondered if real criminals exposed to public humiliation, such as being put in stocks, used the same strategy.

I wish I could tell you that after this painful episode, I returned to school a changed and better boy, but that would be a lie. I stopped acting out and appeared to behave better, but this was just a surface phenomenon. I still hated the school, the teachers, and my anti-Semitic fellow students, and just withdrew into myself and spent most of my class time reading.

PART FIVE
A New Beginning

15

Going to America

Our relatives in the United States, especially my dad's niece Evelyn, tried many subterfuges to speed up getting us to America, but they all failed. First, they tried to get a rabbinical student visa for my father. When this didn't succeed, they found a synagogue that offered him a job as a rabbi. This almost succeeded until the suspicious INS checked out the synagogue and found that they'd already "hired" several hundred other European "rabbis." After a dozen such schemes bore no fruit, we resigned ourselves to wait our turn on the Polish quota.

As the years passed, and our lives in France improved, America became less and less real and the desire to go there lost its desperate edge. When the letter from the American embassy announcing we were now eligible for immigration visas finally arrived, we greeted it with mixed feelings. I was the only family member enthusiastic about the move. Unsure of my future in the French educational system. I needed a fresh start, and going to America was my only hope. My father, not an adventurous soul, saw no reason to abandon a successful business and a comfortable life for all the uncertainties awaiting him in this strange, unknown land. He was fifty-one years old and dreaded the thought of having to start all over again. Had he only known how miserable his first ten years in America would be, my children would be French, and I would write this in the most "civilized" and "literate" language in the world. My mother was the wild card. She'd become accustomed to Paris and liked it, but there was not much challenge left here, and she wanted to ply her talents on a newer and bigger stage. The opportunity to succeed in a new arena won the day, and her determination to conquer America, as she had already conquered France, swamped my father's objections.

Moving to America involved the enormous task of shedding all that my parents had amassed during our six years in Paris. We still didn't have many clothes, but my parents had to find buyers for the apartment and the business, and I had to part with most of my old friends, the books I bought from the bouquiniers with my weekly subway ticket money. One acquisition that my parents planned to get rid of was the baby my mother was carrying. She'd had several abortions over the years, fourteen by her account, but she was prone to exaggeration so it might have been only three or four; I knew nothing about any of them. It may be hard to believe, considering we lived all these years in very close quarters, that I was unaware my parents had sex, which is a required prelude to the need for an abortion. You might ascribe this lack of awareness to my being a sound sleeper, but I opt for the usual reluctance of children to accept the gross idea that their parents have sex.

I knew about one abortion because my mother used it as a cautionary tale of what happens to hoity-toity smart-asses who try to do her ill. She was sitting in her regular abortionist's examination room while he chatted with a distinguished-looking gentleman in his office. Being sharp of hearing and helped by having her ear glued to the office door, she couldn't help overhearing their conversation. The distinguished gentleman asked how much her doctor charged for an abortion, chastised him for charging so little, encouraged him to raise his rate, and assured him his patients would pay whatever he asked; they had no choice.

When her doctor joined her in the examination room, he apologized for having to raise his fee because of higher costs and the increased danger caused by stricter enforcement of anti-abortion laws by the Paris police. My mother took in the news and asked him who his distinguished visitor was. He told her he was a very famous gynecologist with an office on the Champs Elysée. He was also the most expensive abortionist in Paris, his price five or six times greater than she was used to paying. After extracting the visitor's name from the doctor, she told him she had second thoughts about the abortion and went home.

The next day, dressed in her best finery, she made an appointment with the famous doctor, and when he told her his fee, assured him money was no object. She came to him because a physician recommended him as the best in Paris; that was all that mattered. After the abortion, when it came time to pay, she rummaged through her handbag and apologized to her wonderful doctor. Deciding to have an abortion was such a traumatic experience. She didn't know where her head was and had forgotten to bring her wallet. If he could forgive her and drive her home, she would pay him there.

She had to wait till he finished his office hours. He drove her to the hotel Francia where she got out and told him she wouldn't pay him a penny. She hoped this would teach him not to encourage others to gouge money from poor, desperate women. She wanted him to think of her as God's instrument, warning him about the evils of greed. The doctor was furious, indignant, and threatened her with many dire consequences if she didn't give him the money. "I gave him my Mona Lisa smile," my mother said, "and then told him to go to the police if he felt cheated. I left him sputtering while I went into the hotel, like a lady, with my head held high. This is the comeuppance that happens to big shots who try to match wits with Evelyn Fryd."

When I overheard the discussion about the upcoming abortion, I realized how badly I wanted a sibling. I did not know why, but I believed an extra member would transform us into a "real" family. We would all like each other and spend time together like my friends' families, instead of a pair of adults locked till death in mortal bickering, and a lonely kid trying to stay out of the line of fire. I knew my fantasy would never come true, but the thought of a brother or sister was still appealing. He or she represented a chance to have someone I could be close to.

Inspired by this glorious vision of future family life, I raised holy hell and threatened to report my parents to the police if they went through with the abortion. My parents knew the emptiness of my threats, and weren't people who gave in, even on minor points, to the whims of a child, yet they changed their minds. They didn't go through with the abortion and had the child who turned out to be my brother, Marty. I think on some level they saw it as part and parcel of a new beginning, a new child in the new promised land.

16

The Golden Country

My parents sold the apartment and the business as a package deal and forced me to prune my cherished books to what could fit in one valise. We took the train to Le Havre, where we boarded our ship in a state of high excitement. We carried three valises: one for our clothes, one filled with my books, and one carrying our shtetl heritage, a down comforter and a set of bagnkes both indispensable for coping with the cruel Polish winters.

Along with the valises we each carried our own individual hopes and fantasies for our new life in the "Goldene Medineh," the Golden Country, which is what Jews called America, at least until they got there and found out the streets were paved with pyrite (fool's gold) and not the real thing. My fantasies about the United States were all based on American movies, and I expected to land either in the middle of a western or, at worst, a musical. I rooted for the western. At that stage of my life, I found horses and guns far more appealing than girls, no matter how well they sang and danced. My parents' hopes were far more realistic, but they didn't come any closer to becoming true than mine. They expected to wind up in Los Angeles, where my dad's oldest sister, Rivkah, promised to set them up in a small business. My mother had no doubts that, with her talents, this would be a foundation on which she'd build a fortune. America was so much richer than France, and the opportunities for tweaking the system had to be so much more profitable.

In Le Havre we boarded the USS George Washington, a large passenger ship that had seen better days but still tried to keep up pretensions. We didn't spot the genteel shabbiness; for us, the ship looked the height of luxury, at least the upper decks which we inhabited during the day. At night we retired below deck to steerage where men and women slept eight to a room on narrow metal bunk beds in separate, cramped staterooms.

I went to sleep the first night filled with excitement. I felt great and wondered about all these seasickness fairy tales I'd heard so much about. The next morning, I learned how all too real they were as soon as I slid off my bunk. Wave after wave of nausea hit me, but I had to wait my turn for an opportunity to vomit out the only porthole in the stateroom. We were all deathly sick and spent the first couple of days gathered at the railings, giving up the contents of our stomachs. I ate nothing those two days; the thought of food only aggravated the nausea, and I hoped America lived up to its press to warrant suffering this horrible ordeal. Like everything else in life, good or bad, in time the seasickness went away, and we settled down to the normal rhythm of life on board.

The passengers on the USS Washington, all immigrants, represented an ironic bimodal distribution: half were Germans who boarded the ship first, in Bremen, and occupied all the public spaces with no intention of sharing them with the rest, and the other half were Polish Jews, like us, who came on board in Le Havre. There was nothing subtle about the Germans' intentions as they occupied the ship as if it was Europe in 1939. They tried to bully us, pushed, shoved, threatened to finish the job Hitler started, but there were too many of us for them to get their way. The boat became divided into separate parts. The two groups gathered on different decks, ate in separate dining rooms, and exchanged venomous curses and insults at a safe distance from each other.

Once I recovered from my bout of 'mal de mer,' as the French call it, I threw myself into life on board, assuming it represented what life would be like in America. I couldn't have been more wrong if I tried, but this interlude was a pleasant transition before we had to deal with the harsh realities of our first few years in our not-so-golden destination. We would have been better prepared for our later disappointments if we had taken to heart our waiter's dire warnings about life in America, but it is hard to take seriously a message from a stock comic character. He was a classic escapee from a delicatessen on the Lower East Side of New York, a short, stooped man whose slow shuffle testified to feet worn down by thousands of days spent carrying food to unworthy and ungrateful diners. His face twisted into a mask of painful resentment towards the ulcers ravaging his stomach and the unfairness of life that caused them; he had very few illusions and wanted to disabuse us of any we might have.

"Why are you ordering steak?" he scolded. "You greenhorns think you will eat steak in America? Hah! You'll be lucky if you have enough bread. Don't get used to this fancy food." He growled and tried to grab our plates before we took a bite. After a few meals with our resident Cassandra, we learned if we wanted to finish our meal, we had to eat with one hand while clutching the plate with the other.

After seven days at sea, we arrived in New York. My father woke me up at six in the morning. We dressed and went on deck to see the ship pass the Statue of Liberty. I had seen too many great monuments in France to be impressed and was too cold and sleepy to appreciate the symbolism of welcome to the "huddled masses yearning to be free." I couldn't wait to land in our new home and start our exciting new life. Around eight in the morning we docked at the pier and –

wonder of wonders – there was a band ready to welcome us, just like I had fantasized while herding goats during the war, but there was a grotesque twist to the fantasy. It was an Oompah band sent by the New York Bund, a German fraternal organization to welcome not us, but our German shipboard tormentors. It was an apt omen of how much reality would differ from our rosy hopes about our future in America.

We got off the boat on July 23, 1951, clutching our three valises, filled with both hopes and fears about the life awaiting us in this new Promised Land. After processing through immigration, we met my father's two older brothers, Jake and Abe. They had emigrated to the United States when he was still the family's great hope, a little rabbi in training. It was an awkward reunion; they hadn't seen each other in forty years, and the only thing they had in common was the painful loss of parents and siblings slaughtered by the Nazis. We discovered later that they didn't even share a common name. My father kept the original family name (Fryd). The others were told by immigration officials on arrival they were Jake Freed and Abe Fried. Everyone hugged and commented on how much they had changed in the intervening years. We loaded our luggage into Abe's car and drove to his apartment in the Bronx.

Uncle Jake left Poland to save his father from committing filicide when he found him breaking the Yom Kippur fast early, partaking of both a roasted chicken and the neighboring Polish farmer's daughter. Abe followed his older brother two years later. Like most Jewish immigrants of that generation, they wound up working in the garment industry's sweatshops. Jake became a cutter, and Abe, a sewing machine operator. The two brothers were temperamental opposites: Abe was responsible, shy, and very sweet. Jake kept the same bon vivant, rakish character that forced him to leave hearth and home in the old country. He discovered the streets of New York might not be paved with gold, but they were full of young women willing to succumb to his considerable charm.

Jake's long womanizing run ended when he took up with my Aunt Lena. She had four huge brothers who were very protective of their sister's honor. Given the choice of going through life on crutches or doing the right thing, Jake became a husband and, a couple of months later, a father. My mother, wise in the ways of the world, was wont to opine new brides were too inexperienced to know they were supposed to carry their first child for nine months. I heard Jake chafed in both roles, and never lost his taste for blondes. The ever-reliable Abe who remained a bachelor for many years had to step in and support his brother's family while Jake was off consorting with his latest conquest. Jake wasn't an admirable role model, but I loved being around him. I grew up in a family that considered fun and pleasure high on the list of sins to be avoided at all costs. Jake helped me peek into another dimension where one could enjoy such things without guilt or fear of eternal damnation.

As usual, uncle Abe took the family's responsibility on his shoulders, and we moved in with him and his wife, aunt Gussie. Abe, unlike his older brother, was unworldly and shy around women and remained a bachelor till his early thirties. I'm sure it was Gussie, getting past her prime and desperate, who picked him out, decided they should get married, and led him to the altar. For all I know, when young she was an affectionate person, but when we met her, she was a tragic sight: a bitter, angry, depressed specter who wandered aimlessly, railing at the world and Abe. He took it all and tried to calm her by pouring the oil of endless love and kindness on the troubled waters of her soul.

When their son died during the invasion of France, Gussie had a nervous breakdown and never recovered from the loss. It was cruel and thoughtless to have us move in with them. Not only were we intruding on her grief, crowding her in their small two-bedroom apartment, but the sight of my mother pregnant and blooming with good health was an in-your-face reminder of her loss; we were awaiting the birth of a child while she was still mourning the death of hers.

For a while, we were minor celebrities: members of the tribe who survived the Holocaust and were here to tell the tale. My uncles showed us off to countless cousins and unrelated immigrant old timers who, thinking all of Europe was still as primitive as the small Polish villages they left behind, insisted on teaching us how to use the magical modern conveniences in America. They flicked on light switches, flushed toilets, and beamed, expecting us to be awestruck. We disappointed them with our lack of proper enthusiasm, and they ascribed it to the typical backwardness of new immigrants. Still, they wanted to be supportive; they clapped us on the back and assured us we would be fine. "Donne vorry Greenhorns, you gonna be awright. Juss vork hard, donne get in no trouble, and someday you vill be Yehnkees juss like us." We thanked them for the reassurance and avoided telling them we had spent the last six years in Paris, a far more sophisticated place than the Bronx.

A week after our arrival, my father left for Los Angeles to see his oldest sister, Rivkah, who immigrated to the United States soon after he was born. She and her husband settled in Hazleton, Pennsylvania, where starting with a small notions store, they wound up owning several department stores in Wilkes-Barre and Scranton. When her husband died, she and three of her four grown children moved to California. The plan was for us to join them in Los Angeles, where Rivkah, the rich sibling, would help us settle in.

I am not sure why we didn't all go straight to Los Angeles. I assume my parents feared to make an irreversible commitment to California. Their experiences taught them not to rush into things, and to keep a fallback position. It seemed logical for my father to be the scout; my mother was pregnant, and the Californians were his family, but he was the wrong person for this mission. My father, an intelligent man, was devoid of vision and feared change; it took brute force to get him to leave France when the long-awaited visas arrived. The outcome of his scouting trip was predictable: California scared him. It was too different. Used to a life of struggle and denial, he couldn't relate to his family's laid-back expansive lifestyle. A compulsive worrier who looked for dark clouds in every silver lining, he was sure their fantasy world would crash to earth and bury us should we decide to join them in this strange land where even the balmy climate didn't seem real.

His sister's offer to set him up as manager of a bowling alley reinforced my father's negative view of Los Angeles. You had to be crazy to believe "normal" people would pay money to throw a ball at a bunch of wooden pins. Normal was my parents' default evaluative adjective. People who wasted their hard-earned money on drinking, gambling, eating out, and this ridiculous bowling thing, weren't normal: they were stupid. After a three-week stay, my father thanked his sister for her kind offer, and came back to New York, a move he would live to regret. California couldn't have turned out worse than the misery he suffered over the next eight years in New York.

While my father was away, my mother and I went about dealing with our new environment. My mother assessed the stormy emotional climate; she became afraid that while my father was away, Gussie would go off the deep end and throw us out. To minimize this possibility, she went to great lengths to befriend her, and ordered me to be invisible; I could stay in our bedroom or play outside.

A neighbor's son, Allan, introduced me to the kids on the block, and even with my marginal command of English, I realized acceptance required at least two immediate changes. Like all French boys my age, I wore shorts; changing to long pants at sixteen was a major rite of passage, but in 1951, even Bermuda shorts were unknown in the Bronx, and with my uncles' and neighbors' support, I convinced my mother she had to buy me a pair of jeans. The second change was easier. My parents cared little about gentile pseudonyms. They were the figurative masks you wore in the outside world; your only true identity was your Jewish birth name, in my case Moishe, in memory of my formidable paternal grandfather. I had already gone through several names by the time we arrived in the Bronx: I was Mojszesz, the Polish version of Moishe before the war; Mietek, the name on our fake identification papers during the war; and in France I picked Maurice, a good name for a Parisian, but one that smacked of a serious lack of manliness in the Bronx. I abandoned my roots, eschewed the traditional Jewish-American names, starting with M: Morris, Murray, Marvin, Melvin; they all felt wrong. I crossed ethnic lines and chose the more commonly Irish Michael. The nickname Mike sounded tough and feeling insecure in this unfamiliar country where everyone towered over me, I wanted to project a powerful image.

I registered at De Witt Clinton, an all-boys high school that Abe and Gussie's son had attended. Knowing I had one month before school started, I felt pressure to improve my English. Abe and Gussie had only one book in their house, the Pickwick Papers, a remnant of their children's school days. Armed with my trusty English French dictionary, I started translating it. The book contained many useless Victorian words like spats and andirons, but my biggest problem was figuring out how to pronounce the words I learned. There is an abysmal lack of consistency or rationality to English pronunciation rules. Growing up in the United States, you learn by osmosis to pronounce rough and bough differently, and that there is an "r" sound in the middle of colonel. My vocabulary expanded but elicited more laughter than comprehension.

Soon after my father's return, we realized we had to move to our own living quarters. Gussie tolerated our stay as long as it was only a temporary rest stop on our way to the West Coast, but once she saw we weren't moving to California, she wanted us gone. So, two months after our arrival, we moved a dozen blocks south to a one-bedroom apartment on Townsend Avenue. My parents furnished it with the cheapest second-hand furniture they could find: a bed, dresser, wardrobe, and crib for their bedroom, a yellow Formica and chrome dinette set for the kitchen, and a dark green convertible sofa for the living room. The sofa served the dual function of a couch during the day and my bed at night. Some springs uncoiled during its lengthy lifetime and protruded just below the surface of the fabric. I learned not to toss and turn in my sleep and remain immobile once I found a safe spot between the metal points. To this day, I am irritated by people who gush about the elegance of shabby chic decor; poverty is only charming and romantic when you've never had to experience it.

A few weeks after we moved to our own apartment, my two aunts engineered a permanent break between us and the rest of the family. We never understood why they did it. Maybe they feared we'd ask them to help support us. The excuse they used was so preposterous, and their reaction so extreme, we knew they'd planned it. My parents invited them to dinner, and my mother, proud of her culinary skills, went to great lengths to prepare a special meal. The centerpiece was a roasted, rolled up turkey breast. Lena and Gussie decided it was a ham. They wouldn't listen to any denials, or offers to talk to the kosher butcher, who rolled up the offending cut of meat. Even though they weren't very observant, they decided this was a heinous insult, and cut off all communications with us.

The only family it left us with was my mother's half-sister Emma, who was in her late sixties when we came to the United States. You may remember, Emma and her sister Heivet emigrated in their early twenties hoping to find husbands and a new life in America. My grandfather Mendel was too poor to provide a dowry, which made their marital prospects slim. They'd heard a shortage of single immigrant Jewish women made dowries less critical in America and, filled with hope, they set off for El Dorado. Like my uncles, they went to work in the garment industry. The three dollars a week each of them earned couldn't cover both food and lodging, so they begged their employer to let them sleep in the factory, and in return they served as night watch women at no additional pay.

I am not sure when Heivet had a nervous breakdown, but she spent most of her life in a mental institution and died there a few years after our arrival. My mother hinted that Heivet died a virgin and sexual frustration caused the breakdown. Emma was more fortunate; she met and married a somewhat successful singer, with whom she had two children. Her husband died before we arrived in America, and Emma supported herself as a saleswoman in a ladies' clothing store. Though she didn't have my mother's street smarts, she had more energy and lust for life than most people half her age. She worked well into her seventies, standing all day on four-inch heels, which coupled with her tall mane of bright copper-colored curls brought her up to a full five feet. She wore more makeup than was necessary, but it seemed appropriate for her, a natural reflection of her ebullient personality.

Widowhood didn't suit Emma; a determined dater, not a simple task before match.com and Tinder, she walked a fine line in evaluating potential mates, eliminating those who didn't look hearty enough to help her avoid Heivet's fate but rebuking those who tried to take unwarranted liberties. She was interested in sex, but only within the confines of the marital bed. My mother told me these attacks on her virtue occurred far more often than one would expect from social security recipients.

I was privy to our half of a 911 call from Emma while she was fending off one of her dates' amorous advances. My mother was too far away to provide actual physical help, but she was there in spirit if not in body; on her feet, face aflame with fury, she screamed advice and outrage into the phone, while physically playing out her directions for disabling the geriatric Lothario. "How dare he put his hand in your bra! The bastard! Who does he think he's dealing with? Hit him with your shoe!" she yelled as she bashed the air with her own. "What's wrong with these old farts? Punch him in the nose!" A forceful jab strong enough to knock out the offender if he had the misfortune of being in our kitchen instead of Emma's living room. "Kick him in the balls! That will cool off the old goat!" A resolute knee thrust at crotch level.

After Emma pushed the ancient Casanova out of her apartment, my mother slumped into a chair. Covered with sweat, she had trouble catching her breath; but the fight was over, and the two sisters could savor their victory. They went over the date's details. They agreed you could never know about men. There must be something wrong with them. "He acted like such a gentleman all evening, and then just like that, he turned out to be a sex maniac. What gave the pervert the idea he could take such improper liberties, and try to treat Emma like a floozy?"

After refusing to kiss a lot of frogs, Emma met a prince, married him, and they lived contentedly for several years until his death. I understand she went back on the dating scene, but by then I was living out of town and had no access to the details of her love life.

Our apartment was on a block with twenty six-story tenements, each inhabited by forty or fifty families. This kind of population density is hard to imagine for anyone who grew up in a suburban single-family house, but it seemed normal to us. It was a village with all your friends and acquaintances conveniently close. We were one block west of the elevated IRT subway line on Jerome Avenue, a grimy street filled with garages, and small industrial businesses. Our apartment shook every time the train passed by, but after a while we stopped noticing the vibrations and noise. They became a background to our life. Three blocks east was the Grand Concourse: a broad boulevard of upscale apartment houses and shops, the Bronx's combination of Park and Fifth avenues. If you planned to remain in the borough, this was the address you aspired to. Connecting these two, a half a block north of our apartment was Mt Eden Avenue, our neighborhood's downtown. This is where housewives did their daily shopping at the grocery store, delicatessen, butcher shop, fishmonger, and poultry store where you bought a live chicken and five minutes later the butcher kosherly slaughtered and defeathered it. Like most downtowns, it had a movie theater, the Surrey, and several candy stores that served as hangouts for different but loyal groups. I never noticed it at the time, but unlike soda shops in the movies, these were all male clusters.

Once ensconced in our new home, each of us set about our respective tasks: my father tried finding a job as a pocketbook maker, my mother uncharacteristically, but only temporarily, tamped down her entrepreneurial drive and set about feathering the nest for the new arrival, and I focused on adapting to my new school. My father had the hardest job and was the least successful. Every morning at six am he took the subway to the garment district, climbed steep stairs to factory lofts, and with figurative hat in hand asked for a job. Most foremen would look at this small fiftyish greenhorn and dismiss him without even bothering to see if he had any valuable skills. Occasionally they'd give him a chance, but he never lasted over two or three weeks. He was used to being a boss, not a manual laborer, and worst of all, he couldn't adjust to the fast pace expected in America.

For eight years, his work profile was a mountain range of short work peaks separated by long unemployed valleys. He stopped dreaming of getting a permanent job. All he prayed for was twenty weeks of work in a calendar year so he could collect twenty-six weeks of unemployment. I would see him drag himself home every evening, beaten down by unrelenting rejection, and wondered where he found the strength to start all over the next day. It was heroic, not the romantic heroism depicted in books I devoured every spare waking hour where the protagonist gloriously risks and often loses his life for some lofty ideal, but in retrospect it was so much more admirable. There was no glory in his quest, no epic poems praising his bravery, no fair damsels attaching their silk handkerchiefs to his lance as a sign of their love and admiration. It was heroism bred into generations of a reviled and oppressed group, whose only weapon was the ability to endure, and survival the only possible victory. My father wasn't seeking glory; he just wanted a job and the dignity that came with it.

"A man's only job is to earn a living and support his family. If he can't do that, he's a loser, and no one respects him," he lectured me, whenever I broached my desire to become a writer. "Writers are all Luftmenschen (airheads), no normal woman (there goes that damn adjective again) will ever marry a Luftmensch. She'll know her family will starve because the shmendrick won't even think about getting a proper job. It's too late for me, Mietek. I must suffer here because that son of a bitch Columbus couldn't mind his own business and stay home. The bastard had to go look for trouble and discover this miserable country, but you're going to go to college, get a profession, become someone: a doctor, a lawyer, a dentist, be your own boss, someone whom no one can fire. Stop daydreaming and don't squander your opportunity."

At fifteen, I wasn't interested in marriage. My limited sample didn't seem very appealing, but the basic message registered, and became the unexamined but overwhelming driving force of my life; having and keeping a job was not an option, it was a man's manifest destiny, and I was never unemployed for the next sixty years.

While my father continued his Sisyphean struggle against rejection, I set about gaining acceptance from my schoolmates. De Witt Clinton High wasn't quite the Blackboard Jungle, but it was a far cry from the rigid standards and oppressive discipline of an elite Parisian Lycée. I couldn't believe the lack of interest in learning and the rowdiness of my new school. The average grade for my homeroom hovered around 30 out of 100, inflated by the three of us who had passing grades. The other two became my first friends in America; one of them introduced me to my first wife, and the other was the best man at that wedding.

The school's administration wasn't sure how to evaluate my transcript. French schools were meritocratic institutions, uninterested in protecting their students' self-esteem. They graded us against an unreachable ideal. My grades were good enough to place me on the honor roll at the Lycée, if I hadn't disqualified myself by my "abominable" behavior, but they translated to a C minus in the United States. Because of these grades and my limited command of English, they assigned me to "dummy" classes designed to give passing grades to members of our excellent football team. This turned out to be a major break; the guys adopted me, nicknamed me Frenchie, and became my protectors.

The tales of returning soldiers from both World Wars created in America an image of the French as extreme sexual libertines, and my classmates wrongly assumed that since I came from this hotbed of debauchery, I had experienced sex in ways they could only dream of. They peppered me with questions about various sexual practices. Had I tried them? Were they as great as they sounded? Which one did I like best? I'm ashamed to admit that even though I was more ignorant about sex than your typical run-of-the-mill virgin, I didn't disabuse them of their assumptions. Desperate for acceptance, I wasn't about to reject this golden opportunity to appear cool; I acted blasé and assured them I had tried everything they asked about. I even gave "serious" thought to what I liked best; I don't remember my choice. It didn't matter. I was clueless about all of them. Years later, I realized I wasn't the only culprit in these matters; all young men lie about their sexual success, resulting in everyone feeling inadequate. The only difference between myself and the rest was that while every guy thinks there must be something wrong with him since he isn't getting as much as his friends, I wasn't sure what I wasn't getting enough of.

It may seem strange after living for three years in a house of ill repute that I was so ignorant of the essence of my neighbors' trade. I knew people frowned on the profession because the ladies had sex with men who weren't their husbands, but its everyday presence made it no more interesting than the baker or grocer down the street. Contrary to my American classmates' fantasies, my schoolmates and I were inexperienced and ignorant in sexual matters. We had only brief contact with girls; boys and girls went to separate lycées in 1950 and we wouldn't mingle until we arrived at the university. We picked up an approximately correct version of the mechanics of sex on the street and knew from movies and books we would someday become intensely interested in girls. However, at fifteen we were far more invested in the fate of the Racing, a Parisian soccer team, or our favorite bicyclists in the Tour de France, than in the opposite sex.

By the end of the first semester, my teachers realized I was better than my transcript and transferred me to honor classes. At the end of the year, they let me take the New York State Regents examinations in any course I thought I had already taken at the lycée and gave me credit for it when I passed. This enabled me to finish high school in two years and move on to college. My family couldn't afford to pay for a private university, but New York City provided a free college education to students with good grades who could pass the two-day entrance exam for The City College of New York. CCNY opened the road to a better life for generations of working-class immigrant children, hungry bright kids who earned more Nobel prizes than graduates of any Ivy League school.

A month after we moved to our own apartment, I noticed a help wanted sign for a soda jerk at a candy store one block from our house on the corner of Jerome and Mt Eden avenues. Heeding my father's instructions about a man's duty, I applied for the job and the candy store owners hired me at the princely wage of fifty-five cents an hour. The store was next to the train station and had a steady stream of customers picking up newspapers and cigarettes on the way to and from work. Two middle-aged partners, Moe and Joe, ran the candy store, which was profitable, but the real money came from the bookie joint in the back.

I worked every night from six to ten, except on Saturday when my work shift extended to midnight. I loved working there; it was a larger, livelier world unconstrained by the cramped space of our drab little apartment and my parents' cramped worldview. The corner was brightly lit, full of characters who seemed to come straight from the pages of a Damon Runyon short story. Most of them were gamblers who hung around the candy store while they awaited race results, calculated the odds for their next bets, and argued the relative merits of horses and professional or college sports teams. They preferred to bet on the ponies, but worshiped winners and rooted for the New York Yankees and Notre Dame football, the closest things to a sure bet in those days.

I tried to hide the fact that I despised the Yankees, their sense of entitlement and inevitability. I refused to root for the establishment, the haves; we had nothing in common. Instead, I became a passionate fan of the scruffy Brooklyn Dodgers. They might not always win, but they opened doors to outsiders like me; they, not the Yankees, were the first team to bring Black players into the major leagues. Jackie Robinson, given a chance, showed he was as good or better than white players, and fueled my hopes that, given an opportunity, I too might someday prove my worth in my new country.

Like all gamblers, they were extremely superstitious and had intricate routines and talismans they believed guaranteed success. One of the strangest was Harry the Mourner. Harry believed going to funerals brought him luck, and he perused the obituary pages as avidly as the daily racing form. He looked for death notices of people with whom he had some connection, no matter how tenuous. He was ecstatic the day he was "fortunate" enough to attend a first cousin's funeral, convinced he had hit the jackpot. One of his theory's fundamental tenets was this: the closer his relationship to the dearly departed, the greater the luck. That day, he didn't even bother to study the racing form. He bet only on long shots to maximize his guaranteed winnings and spent all day celebrating his upcoming windfall. Unfortunately, none of his horses won. Instead of rethinking his theory, he blamed the losses on his cousin, as useless in death as he had been in life. He was sure the son of a bitch had caused the losses just to spite him.

Another character was Casanova Louie, a jumpy sparrow of a man always in motion but seldom far away from his personal six square feet in front of the candy store. No one knew how Louie supported his large family; he had eight children, while spending all day and evening on our corner. People said he made a living doing odd jobs for the mob and selling goods that conveniently fell off delivery trucks. I saw no evidence of such dealings; maybe they occurred during the day while I was in school. The only thing I witnessed was his wife's frequent, angry visits.

To everyone's amazement, despite his unprepossessing looks and stature, Louie was very successful with neighborhood ladies of a certain age, and often forgot to go home to his wife's loving arms. I don't know why she forgave his serial philandering; maybe she was under the spell of the same mysterious charms that worked so well with his conquests. However, eventually she'd break and storm the corner with fire in her eyes, and unconstrained fury in her voice.

"Louie, you son of a bitch!" she screamed. "How can you abandon us, to shtoop (screw) these kurvehs (whores) who are too ugly to get their own man?" Mrs. Louie, a small woman endowed with a monumental chest that made one wonder how she remained upright, grabbed her husband with one hand while raining blows on his head and face with the other. She cursed the day she met him, cried for the plight of her fatherless children, and dragged him home where I assume there was an eventual loving reconciliation. After each such episode, Louie stayed on the marital straight and narrow for a few weeks, sometimes even months, but eventually he'd succumb again to the allure of new low hanging fruit from the tree of illicit love.

My favorite was Ida, the neighborhood lady of the evening whose office was the coffee shop around the corner. She visited the candy store regularly to feed her addiction to ice cream sodas. This did not help reduce her considerable girth, but caused no problem with her clientele, who liked their women on the zoftig side. Surrounded by gamblers who were always eager for action, Ida occasionally made some extra money by betting on her trade-related skills. Her biggest take occurred the day she beat seven to five odds and stole a sugar dispenser from the coffee shop by hiding it in the tool of her trade. She was an honest woman and, after collecting her winnings, she put the dispenser back on one of the coffee shop's tables. The gamblers drank their coffee unsweetened for a few weeks.

My brother Martin, named Mendel after my maternal grandfather, was born that December. My mother, constrained by a baby's needs, couldn't roam far afield and conduct business as usual, but somehow she kept her hand in. She met a wealthy widower, Mr. Kauffman, who introduced her to the stock market, and guaranteed any losses she incurred by following his stock tips. I assume, like most men, he fell for her and was willing to risk losing money as long as she allowed him to hang around. My mother wasn't classically beautiful, but she controlled the surrounding space by the power of her personality. Sons have a hard time thinking of their parents, in particular their mothers, as sexually attractive beings, but it was impossible to be unaware of my mother's effect on men. She always had a passel of them willing to do anything she wanted, in the vain hope she would leave my father and choose them. My father was furious, but helpless to do anything about her male harems. He had learned long ago he had no control over her actions; all he could do was accuse her of cheating, which earned him angry tirades about his paranoia and general worthlessness.

I grew up observing my mother use these poor souls, and much as I loved and even reluctantly admired her, I developed an uncharitable and cynical, but what I believed to be realistic, view of her actions. I was certain my father's fears were unfounded, not because I thought she had any compunctions about being unfaithful, but because she was too shrewd not to know she had more power if she kept the men hopeful but unsatisfied. She had little respect for men's obsession with sex but was quite happy to use it to her advantage. Sex and its dressed-up version, love, she insisted, when trying to convince me to date random rich girls she dug up for me, had little intrinsic value; like dessert, it was not a cost-effective indulgence. I grew up embarrassed and appalled by what I perceived as an unconscionable exploitation of men's feelings, wondering how my mother could be so callous about love.

One benefit of aging is that the sands of time erode not just monuments, but our most deeply held certainties. They remove layers of carefully maintained personas and expose the truths hiding behind them. I was fifty years old, and my mother was dying of colon cancer. I picked her up after a chemotherapy treatment, and to cheer her up, took her to lunch at a Chinese restaurant. Her face had the waxy yellow look of terminal cancer victims, and her gums had receded, leaving the teeth stranded like unsupported boards in a picket fence. Her cheeks were caved in, and the fire in her eyes that allowed her to dominate any room which she graced with her presence was down to a flicker. She took a few bites of her favorite dish, lobster Cantonese, and stopped. She started sobbing. Used to tears as the first salvo of a campaign to control, manipulate, or even exploit, I stiffened, but then I looked at the shrunken spirit in front of me, and would have given anything to have back the fearsome giant that had dominated my life. We sat quietly for a while. She looked at me longingly and continued sobbing. "I worked so hard all my life... since I was a little girl... nobody was smarter or faster than me... I was the best businesswoman, best housekeeper, best cook… I made a lot of money… I am a valuable woman… and what did it get me? Nothing. All I ever wanted is a little love… for someone to care for me… be tender… hold my hand when we walked down the street." Belatedly, I held her hands and cried with her for all the years she wasted trying to make people love her by showing them what she thought were her best assets: her cunning, resourcefulness, indefatigability, courage, and enormous charm. It got her admiration, but also fear she would use these strengths against them. I wondered how much happier her marriage and our whole family would have been if she had let us see the lonely, vulnerable woman starved for affection; instead, we spent lonely lifetimes separated by walls of fear and anger.

17

Education, Ticket to the Future

Much as I enjoyed the excitement of working at the candy store, I left it to become an usher at the Surrey, the neighborhood movie theater, lured by a twenty cent an hour raise, a significant sum of money in 1952. The job was less exciting, but a lot easier than the candy store. I had to be there to shush the hordes of little kids on Saturday and Sunday matinees, and six evenings a week to restrain the ardor of young couples who sought the privacy provided by the theater's darkness. A year later, management gave me another quarter raise and promoted me to relief manager. I traded the one-size-fit-all usher's jacket and clip-on bowtie for my blue serge high school graduation suit, white shirt, and tie.

The Surrey was part of the J&J chain of movie theaters in the Bronx. I managed The Surrey five nights a week, and The Ascot, the chain's art-house, all-day Thursday from noon to midnight. Saturday was my one night off. My job required very little managing. I was the resident seventeen-year-old "adult" responsible for handling emergencies and restraining the staff from skimming too much money from ticket sales.

The job wasn't arduous but was very time-consuming and, coupled with my lack of enthusiasm for my chosen course of studies, resulted in mediocre college grades. I had given up my dreams of becoming a writer, but I wasn't about to choose one of my parents' only known and, therefore, approved professions: medicine, law, dentistry, or accounting, in that preferred order. I was a teenager who needed to rebel and declare his independence, so I chose chemical engineering. It sounded manly, daring, and it horrified my parents. Engineering was a Gentile profession; who'd ever heard of a Jewish engineer?

I've made a lot of poor decisions in my life, but few were worse and less informed than my choice of engineering as a career. Engineering requires precision and attention to detail; close enough is not only unacceptable but dangerous when you design a process or a plant. Like most people, I have my fair share of strengths, but precision and interest in details are not amongst them. It took me two years to acknowledge defeat and look for alternatives. I didn't know anyone whom I could trust to give me impartial and knowledgeable advice, so I consulted the good folks at Student Services. They gave me a series of aptitude and interest tests. I scored in the 99th percentile in social sciences and humanities, 95th percentile in science, but all the tests showed I was totally unfit for, and uninterested in, engineering.

I loved my "culture for engineers" courses, a compressed compendium of social science and humanities. They were the only classes I enjoyed and excelled in. Armed with my newfound information, I went to inquire from doctor Sas, the professor who taught them, if it was possible to uphold my "manly" duty and earn a living in any of these fields. Professor Sas, a nice scholarly man, must have suffered a brain cramp that day. I knew he liked me. I was the only engineering student who showed interest and enthusiasm in his classes, but he gave me awful advice. He agreed I had aptitude in these areas, thought I was good enough to get a Ph.D. and become a college teacher, but ignoring the reality that many of his colleagues were foreign born, advised against pursuing such a career. He thought my accent made it unlikely any university would hire me.

I couldn't afford the luxury of disappointment or inertia and took what I felt was the only course of action left open to me. As a chemical engineering student, I had taken several chemistry courses; they weren't exciting, but a switch to that major wouldn't delay graduation, and organic chemistry seemed unstructured enough to be tolerable. Reluctantly, I embraced the change that led later to a successful career. Despite my lack of interest in science, I turned out to be very good at it, and I wound up in a fifty-year loveless but companionable marriage with chemistry. I strayed from it a few times and pursued more alluring options, but always came back to the comforts of a generous paycheck, and the guilty pleasure of approval and recognition. Fortunately, unlike my human partners, chemistry was always forgiving and willing to take me back.

While I struggled with work and school, my parents' life improved. My father still didn't have a steady job, but he found work for longer periods. My brother started school, and my mother had the freedom to expand her business activities. Besides Mr. Kauffman, she befriended several stockbrokers and became an expert at evaluating their collective advice. Each thought he was her sole broker and was amazed by her acumen and deep knowledge of stocks. Even though she disapproved of gamblers -- she thought they were moral degenerates -- she loved the rush of betting on the market. However, like most professionals, she didn't depend on luck. She always did her homework and won more than she lost. She became so good at it that, years later, my stockbroker friends wanted to know her recommendations.

Stocks were a profitable sideline, but her principal business became buying overstocked clothes from garment manufacturers and reselling them at a profit to retail stores. She got into this by partnering with yet another man, Mr. Bookbinder, a rotund old elf who emigrated from

Romania. He was always cheerful, and unfailingly kind. All he wanted out of life, besides my mother, was to enjoy three or more cholesterol-laden meals washed down with a few shots of brandy, and a shvitz (steam bath) at the end of his day. He was confident these simple pleasures were his recipe for a long life and loved telling anyone willing to listen how he had buried the doctor who advised him to lose weight, give up fatty foods, and avoid alcohol.

He led a quiet life, and his modest business was profitable enough to satisfy his simple needs. All this changed when my mother became his partner. Dissatisfied with what she considered mediocre profits, she expanded the business into more legally nuanced areas.

The garment industry existed in a state of permanent insecurity. Manufacturers' fortunes fluctuated from season to season, hostage to the ever-changing fashions and capricious tastes of buyers. Every year, many of them went broke and needed to convert their stock into cash before declaring bankruptcy. Some, greedy or just devoid of even a minimum amount of moral fiber, suffered opportune fires, and insurance companies covered their losses. I don't know how my mother got advance notice of these planned misfortunes, but it gave her leverage. And she could bring her cost down to five to ten cents on the dollar. Sometimes it took months to sell it all, but the profit margins were exceptional. In all these dealings, as she did with stolen goods after the war, my mother felt on solid moral ground. She refused to take any responsibility for others' misdeeds. Her part of the transaction was always legitimate. She purchased goods with honest money, and it was not her job to worry about her providers' sins.

My parents' improved fortunes led to a significant upgrade in our creature comforts. A new gray convertible sofa that opened into twin beds replaced the dangerous green couch. I shared it with my brother. A matching armchair and a television set complemented the couch. To protect these precious new possessions, my mom covered them with both dark brown cloth, and clear plastic slipcovers. It took forever to remove all the layers and open the couch before going to bed, but it was such an improvement I wasn't about to complain.

During my college junior year, I finally got to experience the lies I laid claim to with my high school classmates. There were few women in my engineering and science classes, and my nightly work schedule left me with little free time. Friends arranged a few dates, but I was too shy and inexperienced, and they all ended after the first date. I was lonely and decided it was time for a change. I knew I couldn't make my shyness disappear, but I could force myself to hide it and show the world a poised and confident exterior. It surprised me how well the act worked. I didn't have my mother's natural theatrical flair, but I committed to the role wholeheartedly, and it became easier and more comfortable with time. I stopped needing friends to set me up, got first and repeat dates on my own, and eventually halfway through my junior year I met Helen, who wasted little time introducing me to her bed and the wonders of her practiced body.

Helen, as I found out later, was crazy every month, not just March, like Lewis Carroll's Hare. She gave me more pleasure and pain than I'd experienced till then, and maybe even since. Early in our relationship, Helen confided she was suffering a terminal illness, and stayed alive the last two years thanks to an experimental treatment. Unfortunately, according to her doctor, the prognosis was poor, and she probably had only eighteen months left to live. My world collapsed; I had met the love I had longed for all these years, and I was going to lose her. We would never live happily ever after. I had little experience with run-of-the-mill boy meets girl relationships but lived and cried with endless doomed literary love stories for years. This was familiar ground; a tragic love story so much nobler than the trite Sandra Dee/Troy Donahue romances playing in the movies. Helen's impending death made me love her even more. I wanted to spend every remaining minute with her. My work schedule left me free only on Saturday nights, so I cut classes to be with her, which only exacerbated my already mediocre record. We became engaged over the objections of her parents, who thought me too low class for their taste. Her stepfather was a successful corporate accounting executive, and unlike me, a newly arrived immigrant, her parents were both fourth generation Americans.

Several friends suggested Helen was friendlier with fellow male students than one might expect of an engaged woman. I refused to listen to a word against her. They didn't know she had only months to live and didn't understand the depth of our love. Still, I wondered why she was never home when I called her from work; she was out with a girlfriend, visiting her aunt, studying late at the library. There was always a good reason, but after a while doubt started nibbling at the edges of my absolute trust.

One night, when once again she wasn't home when I called, I deserted my post at the movie theater, overwhelmed with jealousy and determined to find out what was really happening. I told the staff I was sick, delegated my responsibilities to the doorman, and walked over to her house. I hid in a doorway across the street and prayed for my vile suspicions to be unfounded. It was December. I hadn't bothered to grab my overcoat, and I was shaking both from the cold and fear of what I might see. Around one am, I saw her walk around the corner; she wasn't alone, she was walking with another guy, their arms wrapped around each other's waists. They stopped in front of her building and kissed for a long time, their bodies intertwined. My body shook uncontrollably. I wanted to run away but feared she would see me. It would complete my humiliation. I stayed and watched them paw each other. Eventually they separated; she went into her building, and he walked away humming a show tune. When he was gone, I stumbled home, threw myself on the bed, and cried. It took a while to calm down and move from numbness to resolve. This would never happen again; nothing was worth this much pain. I would let no one hurt me like that again. I let this resolve crumble many times in the ensuing years, not because I had a poor memory or a masochistic strain, but because my desire to love and be loved was greater than my fear of pain.

I confronted Helen the next day. She denied everything, but I had witnessed her betrayal. Our engagement was off. I walked away with a raw, pain-wracked heart, but my steps were lighter unburdened by the weight of doubt and jealousy. Once my friends knew I'd broken up with her, they felt free to stop hinting and let loose with all they knew. Helen had been fooling around with an endless number of partners. She favored members of the college ROTC, and a year later, instead of dying a tragic death, she got pregnant, married the supposed father, and became an army wife.

One of our weekly family rituals was the Thursday evening scan of help wanted ads in the Women's Wear Daily. If any of them even remotely matched my father's qualifications, I typed a letter describing my father's experience and skills before going off to work. It was like playing the lottery; you don't really expect to win, but you keep playing because if you ever did win, it would change your life. We never received a response until one day, after eight years of fruitless effort, my father got an interview for a job at a handbag factory in Wilkes-Barre, Pennsylvania. The owners ran a trucking business in the garment district; we suspected they belonged to The Mafia, which controlled that part of the garment industry, and set up the handbag factory to launder their money.

They knew nothing about handbags and needed someone to run the plant. My father fit their needs perfectly; he was mature, responsible, and had run his own mini factory in Paris. After years of sporadic employment, my father finally had a steady, responsible job that allowed him to show his considerable talents. He rented a room in Wilkes-Barre and took a bus home on weekends. Eventually, this became too hard. He bought a car and learned to drive at sixty-five. He was an overly cautious driver, but how many of us have the courage, initiative, and determination to learn a complex new skill at that age?

My father came to work at six in the morning and didn't leave until late in the day. He ran the plant as if it was his own, saved every penny he could in labor and materials, and as an unexpected bonus created original and distinctive designs that became popular with buyers. Under his management, to his bosses' surprise, the factory designed to launder illicit gains made substantial profits. I can't say my father was finally happy; happiness wasn't an emotion I ever associated with him, but for the first time in many years, he wasn't visibly unhappy. It wasn't much, but I was relieved and thrilled for him. However, the years spent wandering hopelessly in the unemployment desert left deep scars. No matter how much his bosses praised him and how many raises they gave him, he never felt secure in his job. He refused to take a vacation, afraid they'd replace him while he was gone. He stuck to his guns, wouldn't take a day off, and reluctantly retired at seventy-five only when the factory closed.

At the end of my senior year, all my scholastic sins came to a head: my workload, the classes I cut to be with Helen, and my lack of passion for chemistry left me three courses short of the required number for graduating with my class. I planned to finish those courses in the evening and found a day job working at a research laboratory run by the chemical engineering department at NYU. The laboratory staffed with chemistry graduate students worked on contracts to develop advanced rocket fuels for the Navy. They paid us meager wages for doing sophisticated and extremely dangerous research. Rocket propellants are powerful explosives, either by themselves or mixed with other chemicals. Small quantities of air, moisture, heat, or even mild shock triggered uncontrolled explosions and many of the chemicals used to produce the fuels were extremely toxic. Almost everyone working in the laboratory suffered an injury, some serious enough to require hospitalization. I avoided that fate but, always an overachiever, blew the roof off of a building used to scale up promising new materials.

The Navy became interested in a molecule I had synthesized with a senior colleague. They thought it might be an excellent candidate as a fuel for the Polaris missile and asked us to make fifty pounds. It was the minimum needed to conduct more extensive tests. We'd never made over two ounces in the laboratory, but ignorant of the problems we were likely to encounter, and filled with unwarranted confidence, we took on the task. The molecule was stable as long as we kept it at a temperature below one hundred degrees Fahrenheit, so we ran the scale up in a fifty-gallon reactor whose internal temperature we controlled by the speed of cold water running through metal coils wrapped around its exterior. We spent the whole day monitoring the temperature and adjusting the water flow to stay in the safe range. By nine pm, we thought the reaction was over, and it was safe to go home. I was lying in bed watching the eleven o'clock news, when to my horror I heard a bulletin announcing an explosion on NYU's Bronx campus. There were fearful speculations that the explosion came from a recently installed experimental atomic reactor, but I knew better, threw on my clothes and ran back to the campus. The explosion was so strong it blew off the roof seventy-five feet above the reactor. We had done everything right but didn't expect a drop in water pressure that allowed the temperature to rise above the safe range.

To our surprise, the department chair didn't fire or even chastise us. Maybe he had trouble recruiting new 'suicide' chemists. He told us the Navy still needed its fifty pounds, and he expected us to produce them. The department installed a new reactor and this time, we took no chances and stayed through the night until we were sure the reaction stopped giving off heat.

All of us worked in that laboratory, heedless of the dangers we faced because they were such a normal part of our daily routine and because the job had significant benefits. Many of the researchers/students were married with families to support, and this was the only viable path towards a Ph.D. available to them. We had time to gain invaluable experience working independently on complex projects, got free graduate school tuition, and had the flexibility to leave the laboratory for classes, if we made up the time.

I finished my three remaining courses in the fall semester, and applied to NYU's graduate chemistry program, hoping against hope my work at the laboratory would make up for my abysmal scholastic record. Unfortunately, the graduate committee refused to see it that way. My mother called me at work during lunch hour and read the letter from NYU. The school was sorry, but based on my grades, I wasn't proper material for their Ph.D. program.

The bad news wasn't unexpected, but still devastating. I wasn't ready to spend my life being a low-level technician, and for the first of many times when I found myself in an untenable situation, I asked myself WWMD (What Would Mom Do). I had observed her for years. Channeling her is both instinctive and easy, but I reserve it only for the direst predicaments; I try to use it sparingly, and only for good. This calamity fit the bill. I put the phone down, told my boss I had to take the afternoon off, and rode the subway to NYU's downtown campus, home to the graduate school. I found the Dean's office and told his secretary I needed to see him. It was impossible; he had meetings all afternoon and would come back to his office only to pick up his coat and briefcase on the way home. Would I like to make an appointment for some time later in the week?

I thanked her, told her I preferred to take my chances and wait till he came back. I ignored her annoyed assurances my wait would be fruitless, sat down, and waited. The Dean came back around five o'clock. His secretary told him about the importunate young man who'd been sitting there for four hours and refused to leave without seeing him. My persistence may have impressed the Dean, or maybe he just felt sorry for me, but he agreed to give me five minutes. I wasted no time and told him I understood why NYU rejected me, that I would have done the same in their place, but I was far smarter than my grades suggested, and all I asked was permission to take two graduate courses to prove my point. I was confident I would get A's in them. If I didn't, I would never bother him again, but if I did, would the school reconsider my application, or, at least, let me keep taking courses? I'm not sure whether the Dean agreed because my determination, or my chutzpah, impressed him, but he signed off on the courses.

I got A's in the two courses and took the next four on probation. My near-death academic experience scared me enough to abandon all reservations about chemistry. I couldn't afford the luxury of obsessing about a lack of interest in the subject. A Ph.D. in chemistry was my ticket out of the Bronx, and as my parents often said, "We're talking about work. Earning a living. What does enjoyment have to do with it?"

I moved out of the house, overcoming my parents' objections by pointing out the obvious: it was impossible to study in our crowded and noisy one-bedroom apartment. I rented a small furnished room near the university and set about mastering my future profession. The room was part of a six-bedroom apartment owned by a dark-haired, fleshy woman of a certain age. Her husband, a traveling salesman, was seldom home, and she spent her days in an enormous bed, her majestic bosom spilling out of a black negligee that did little to hide her dubious charms. She hinted broadly she'd lower my rent if I joined her there. Thanks to Helen, I had lost my virginity and discovered the pleasures of sex, but I clung to my romantic illusions. I still dreamt of running in slow motion through a field of wildflowers, Beethoven's Pastoral symphony playing softly in the background, my arms outstretched towards a delicate girl with long flowing hair, dressed in a pastel-colored muslin dress, who was running towards me. I wanted to be in love, not just rut. I declined the offer as gracefully as I could, claiming that tempting as it was, I was engaged and felt obligated to remain faithful to my fiancée. Some or all the other four tenants, all men, must have been more obliging; lusty screams coming from her bedroom when her husband was away often kept me awake.

My room was so small it could accommodate only a single bed, a small dresser, and a little table and chair under the window that served as my desk. In winter, bitter cold permeated through the leaky window, making it impossible to stay warm. I went to bed wearing all my clothes, including my parka, but it wasn't enough to stop me from shivering under the covers. Still, I was more than willing to overlook these discomforts; for the first time in my life, I was master of my domain, free from unwanted intrusions into my introverted reveries. There were no distractions, human or electronic, and I could concentrate on studying. A judicious amount of fear is a powerful motivator; I was determined to never again give up control of my destiny to the whims of strangers.

Like all my fellow students, I felt extreme pressure. Unlike college, we only had one exam per course. It and it alone determined our grade. My adviser promised me a National Science Foundation Fellowship if I got at least a B in my advanced organic chemistry class. I could give up my job and concentrate on research for my dissertation. I took three weeks off from work, studied from early morning till late at night, and felt confident when I entered the exam room. The professor gave us the exam, five questions, at eight in the evening and told us we had till eight the next morning. When finished, we were told to slip the exam booklet under his office door. I panicked when I read the questions. None of them looked familiar. Not only would I not get the fellowship, but this would also end my tenure in graduate school. How could I stay if I got a zero in the key course in my field of choice? I was hysterical for a couple of hours until I finally accepted my fate, lit a cigarette, and started considering career alternatives.

Resignation brought calm, and when I glanced again at the exam, I realized I knew the answer to one question. I would still fail, but at least I wouldn't suffer the disgrace of a zero. I leisurely answered that question and noticed I also knew the answer to one more. Thank God! It wouldn't be a total disaster. Slowly, one by one, I answered all the others. I finished at four in the morning so charged up I could light up a medium-sized village. Don Yee, one of my coworkers at the laboratory, finished with me. We both knew we couldn't go home in this state. There was a major blizzard blanketing New York, and only mad dogs and graduate students would dare venture out in such weather. We wandered through deserted streets, whipped by the wind and hard driving snow, but felt nothing. We needed to keep moving.

Don, married with two children, was shivering, and kept repeating, "Why am I putting myself through this? I don't need this! My father-in-law is the Chinese noodles king. He wants me to quit graduate school and come work with him in Boston." I didn't know how to answer him and wasn't sure he wanted me to; he might be just venting. After a couple of hours, frozen and exhausted, we said goodbye to each other and stumbled home. Don disappeared from the job and school a week after the exam. I don't know if he passed or failed, but assumed he took up his father-in-law's offer, and wished him well. Unlike him, I didn't have a handy Plan B, so I waited anxiously for the results. Fortunately, I got a ninety-five on the exam, an A for the course, and the much-coveted fellowship.

18

Not Yet Yehnkees, but Americans

I would take occasional breaks from work and study and go off with Herbie, my first and best friend in the United States. We met in homeroom at De Witt Clinton and remained inseparable, even during the four years he spent out of town at New Paltz State College. We slummed through Greenwich Village bars, but always finished the night at the Cedar Street Tavern, which I found out later was famous as a hangout for avant-garde artists. We shared our inebriated dreams late into the night, and assured each other we were different, and so much more sophisticated than the stodgy "bourgeois" Jewish milieu that birthed us. Someday we would move out of the Bronx, and unlike our parents, lead exciting and adventurous lives. We were too young and fatuous to realize there was nothing original about disdain for our parents' lives; people our age had done and said these things since the beginning of time, and their children echoed the same sentiments about them.

Herbie told me he was gay during his junior year in college. He didn't use that term since in 1960 it implied merriment, not sexual orientation. This took me aback for a moment. I had heard about homosexuality, mostly through snide and derogatory jokes, but stored it in the space reserved in my brain for unicorns and millionaires, mythical creatures I never expected to encounter. However, I recovered quickly. This was still Herbie, my best friend. It changed nothing, just added a tinge of exotic to his already large personality.

Herbie was an artist, but until the world discovered his talent, he supported himself by teaching art in a suburban middle school. It turned out to be a terrible choice; middle school boys are cruel members of our species. They give up pulling wings off flies and take up instead the torture of any vulnerable creature they spot in their midst. I always enjoyed Herbie's flamboyant tendencies and ascribed them to his artistic temperament. His students came to a different but more accurate conclusion and tortured him with catcalls and posters on the school walls depicting him in various sex acts with men.

Herbie, caught between the daily harassment by this army of midget Torquemadas, and relentless pressure from his parents to get married and produce grandchildren, cracked. He told me communists were spying on him and passing coded messages about him on the radio. I was unsophisticated about mental illness and tried to convince him he was just imagining things. He thought I was part of the conspiracy and stopped talking to me. I would give anything to have the same professional knowledge then that I have now, or that his torment occurred ten years later after the Stonewall rebellion. My poor friend could have gotten proper support both from both me and the insurgent gay community; but he didn't, and committed suicide at twenty-five.

I was fine working at the laboratory by day and studying chemistry nights and weekends. It became a familiar routine. Marty, my other high school homeroom friend, disturbed this tranquil monastic existence one Sunday afternoon. He'd fallen head over heels for a girl he'd just started dating. He wanted to take her out that afternoon, but she wouldn't go out with him unless he found a date for her friend

Judy. She'd promised to spend the day with her and couldn't just dump her to go out with him. I was his only hope; everyone else he knew had a girlfriend. It would only be one afternoon; I never had to see the girl again. I was tired of studying, felt the desperation in his voice, and agreed to take one for a friend.

Judy turned out to be a pleasant surprise when they picked me up. I had steeled myself for the worst, but she turned out to look like a blond Elizabeth Taylor and was charming and smart to boot. I've always been a weak vessel, easily influenced by good looks, so it was no surprise I continued seeing her. She was nineteen, a sophomore at my alma mater CCNY, and I was a very young twenty-two. The relationship progressed and after a few months, the mores of the time dictated we had to get married. It turned out to be a false alarm, but by then it was too late. We were married by a Justice of the Peace with Herbie as the best man and our only witness.

Judy and I were terribly young and immature, unprepared for dealing with this new reality. We told no one and continued living apart for a month, but eventually, we had to face the fact that, ready or not, we were married, and God knows we weren't ready. Our after-the-fact announcement to friends and relatives met with mixed reviews, but we were relieved. It was easier dealing with a scary unknown than living in limbo. Judy's parents insisted on a grand wedding reception that rivaled the one in Philip Roth's Goodbye Columbus for both excess and poor taste. They spent a small fortune on it, money we could have used to survive the next few years, but that was not an option.

We started married life in a one-bedroom apartment in the no-man's-land between two ethnic enclaves. The West Bronx, like Gaul, was divided into three parts: Jewish, Italian, and Irish. Our building was on the dividing line between the Jewish and Italian neighborhoods, integrated by Bronx standards. The ethnic mixing caused no tensions, only an occasional cultural misunderstanding, such as the Italian grocer on the corner who, at Easter time, put kosher for Passover stickers on bread, and couldn't understand why we still wouldn't buy it. We furnished the apartment with our wedding gift money but kept five hundred dollars as an emergency fund we nursed religiously. Judy was still in school, and we had to subsist on the hundred and seventy-five dollars a month from my National Science Foundation Fellowship.

The building was old, and we had to share our apartment with a host of cockroaches. Our limited budget allowed only a modest allocation for insecticide, so we learned to coexist. They swarmed the apartment when it was dark, and ceded ground when the lights went on. Our only other problem was the elderly Italian widower who lived above us. He loved to listen to opera while soaking in his bathtub. We didn't mind the music, but it put him to sleep. He would forget to turn off the taps, and water would stream through the ceiling into our apartment. We learned to run up the stairs the moment we heard the first aria and bang on his door to wake him before the bathtub overflowed.

The transition to full-time graduate studies was not as easy as I expected. For two years, I took courses, studied for exams, got good grades, and could ignore chemistry the rest of the time. Now I, a chemical agnostic, who only wanted a union card that would open doors to a good job and a world beyond my ethnic ghetto, found myself thrust into a world where the faculty expected me to be a true believer who not only felt but exhibited religious fervor towards the Gods of Science. Toiling in the laboratory twelve hours a day, six or more days a week, wasn't enough. They expected me to view the world as a vast wasteland dotted by universities and research centers. The only things that mattered were the research programs conducted in these scientific enclaves who communicated with each other through peer-reviewed scientific journals.

While everyone else in the world worried about trifling concerns, like the cold war and possible destruction of humanity by the atom bomb, I was supposed to care only about the raging controversy between two schools of thought on the presumed structure of a minor family of carbon-based ions. The passion and tortured logic poured into what I secretly believed was an intellectual fine point, were reminiscent of scholastic arguments about how many angels could dance on the head of a pin. The hundred-year religious wars had nothing on this mortal struggle. No one burned the heretics at the stake, but their fate in the academic milieu was no less grim: tenured professors insulted each other in scientific journals and at conferences, and more vulnerable younger scientists didn't get tenure for not adhering to the same set of beliefs as the rest of their department.

I didn't love science when I started graduate school, but believed it was governed by logic, which rendered it immune to the usual subjective distortions common to other human activities. I discovered, watching this quasi-religious war, that while science's goal is the search for universal truths, imperfect human beings carry out the task. Eventually truth wins out, but the process, like making sausage, is ugly. This wasn't my first or worst experience with disillusionment; nothing compared to discovering at twelve that my father could tell a lie. I had long ago accepted my mother's flexible attitude towards the truth. I knew, like all talented artists, she needed her medium to be malleable enough to allow her to shape it into a masterpiece, but I depended on my father to be my compass, and reality check; discovering he too could lie left me adrift with nothing solid to cling to.

Discovering that science, unlike Ivory soap, wasn't even close to being 99.4 percent pure, didn't change my determination to get a doctorate. That goal was always based on practical rather than idealistic considerations. I put my head down, studied hard, put in endless days and often nights doing research for my dissertation and, when necessary, faked enthusiasm. It was a grueling, stressful process, but it helped to share it with others. While a few true believers were prepared to join the scientific priesthood, and pursue high-level academic research, most of us just wanted to finish and get a nine-to-five job that would allow us to lead the good life. We were all overworked, barely survived on our meager wages, and shared common dreams of the future when we finally graduated. As tough as things were for us, we knew it could be worse. Half of the physical chemistry students were Indian graduates of Bombay University. Each month they sent forty dollars, a quarter of their wages, to the wives and children they left behind. They shared small apartments and survived on curries cooked on Bunsen burners in their laboratories. Their only extravagance was chain-smoking off-brand cigarettes.

We became a tightly knit group, supported the unfortunates whose research proved to be a dead end, and had to start again from scratch, or even worse those whose advisers kept them well beyond the usual four or five years, forcing them to keep grinding out material for papers that enhanced the professor's reputation. The truly sad cases were told after three or four years they were not Ph.D. material and sent away with a Master's degree. Fortunately, there were also joyous occasions when one of us jumped through the last hoop and successfully defended his dissertation. We celebrated with a blowout party, and actual brand name liquor instead of diluted 180 proof alcohol stolen from the laboratory stockroom. We kept the booze out of sight for fear of a jinx until the dissertation committee came out and congratulated the new doctor.

However, even those who finally succeeded found reality didn't always match their expectations. One of my lab mates, Sal Megna, came from a blue-collar Italian family. He kept reassuring his worried and embarrassed widowed mother that when he got his PhD, he would get a better job than anyone in the neighborhood and show her friends that he went to graduate school to become a professional, not because he was too lazy to get a job. When he graduated, and one of the larger chemical companies hired him, he bought an Alfa Romeo convertible and drove it round and round the neighborhood to show off his success. Unfortunately, no one in the neighborhood had ever seen an

Alfa Romeo; successful people drove Cadillacs. They pityingly told his mom they were sorry that after all these years in school, Sal got such a poor job he couldn't afford to buy a full-size car. We all laughed nervously when he told us the story, but it cast a foreboding shadow on our own sunny plans.

While I plodded my way toward a Ph.D., my mother expanded her activities beyond the borders of the United States. We became US citizens, and she could now travel abroad without fear of not being allowed back. Her first few trips were to Israel to visit her oldest brother, Josef, his son Chaim, and her sister, Sarah. Sarah, her husband, and children escaped across the border to Russia ahead of Hitler's hordes. They may have escaped certain death in a concentration camp, but the five years spent in a Siberian Gulag were only a bit better. Only the strongest and most determined survived the forced labor, extreme cold, and starvation. When we saw them in Warsaw after the war, they were like deer in winter, relentlessly focused on foraging for food. They bought all the bread they could afford and carry; no one could convince them bakeries would have bread the next day. They survived by giving up illusions and hopes, trusting only in what they could get that day.

Sarah spent several years in a Displaced Persons camp in Germany and emigrated to Israel in 1948 when it became a state, while Josef and Chaim went to Palestine in 1939, planning to bring their families over once they felt settled. Unfortunately, by the time they were ready, Germany invaded Poland, their families were trapped and died in concentration camps. Like Mr. Yanofsky, separated from his wife and children by the closure of the Russian border, they never remarried. Their losses remained open wounds that festered till the day they died.

My mother was eager to see these remnants of her once large family, but also wanted to ensure her trip was cost effective. She researched the goods in greatest demand on the Israeli black market, and departed with two valises full of transistor radios, Parker fountain pens, and bottles of Chanel No. 5 perfume. When questioned by customs, she insisted these were gifts for her countless relatives and friends in Israel. From what I gathered later, the sale of the 'gifts' resulted in a net profit for the trip.

On a subsequent trip, she spotted a much bigger opportunity. She discovered through her unique intelligence system Israel had to import steel wool, and fortuitously, a Jewish family owned a steel wool manufacturing equipment company in the United States. An inveterate matchmaker, she saw a marriage made in heaven. First, she struck a deal with the Israeli labor ministry; she would provide the machinery if they put up a building to house it. Then she contacted the machine manufacturers in Connecticut, told them about the Israeli government's plight, forced to squander precious foreign currency to import steel wool. She reminded them every Jew was obliged to support the fledgling Jewish state; our only refuge should there be another Holocaust. Her hosts, swayed by her eloquence, agreed not only to donate the equipment but also to pay for its transportation to Israel. Without investing a penny of her own, my mom became half owner of a factory that became a reality thanks to her opportunistic foresight and inspired negotiating skills. Years later, she traded that half interest for a chewing gum factory. I lost the subsequent transaction trail after a while, but I'm sure the chewing gum factory eventually morphed into some new lucrative enterprise.

In the spring of 1961, my advisor reluctantly agreed I'd done enough work. He allowed me to look for a job while I wrote my dissertation. Mentally exhausted from four years of twenty-four/seven immersion in research, I didn't think I wanted to spend the rest of my life doing more of the same. This helped rule out jobs in industry and research-oriented high-powered universities. I didn't feel emotionally equipped to prosper in those environments. I thought they would require rigor and passion for science, two qualities I sorely lacked. Like many of my other personal insights, I was dead wrong. I wound up spending most of the next fifty years flourishing in both environments, despite these personal deficiencies. I thought I'd be happiest and best off as a professor at a small, teaching-oriented college, and sent out resumes to every school in the New York metropolitan area. Like all true native or adopted New Yorkers, the thought of leaving the center of the "known" universe never even crossed my mind.

After a couple of months of increasingly nervous waiting, Long Island University offered me $4200 per year. I was ready to accept it; fortunately, Judy suggested I call the schools that hadn't responded yet before I made a final decision. The chair of the chemistry department at Hunter College was glad to hear from me. He planned to invite me for an interview, and we set up an appointment for the next day. Judy accompanied me to Hunter's Manhattan campus and waited for me in the lobby.

I met with him and several department members. We discussed my thoughts about future research and why I wanted to teach. After an hour, the chair asked me to step out for a minute while he discussed my fate with his colleagues. He called me back in, told me I'd impressed everyone, and offered me a position at $6300 a year. He misunderstood my stunned silence for disappointment and suggested we visit the Dean. If she liked me, he could raise the offer to $6700. The chit chat with the Dean went well. She approved the additional four hundred dollars. I recovered and, afraid that this too good to be true offer was just a mirage, accepted enthusiastically before it disappeared. On the way back to his office, the chair mentioned the offer was really $7000 because everyone was getting a $300 raise in the fall.

Over the years, I received many job offers and raises orders of magnitude larger, but none came close to being as meaningful and thrilling as that one. After saying goodbye to the chair, I ran down to the lobby and, too choked up to speak, grabbed Judy and danced her around the room. It took me a while to regain my voice and tell her the miraculous news. Overcome by an emotional tsunami, we must have looked like a pair of crazies to students and faculty strolling through the lobby. We alternated between whoops of joy and uncontrollable crying. Our years of subsisting on the ragged edge of poverty were over; we felt rich beyond the boundaries of our limited financial imaginations.

We decided this transition into a prospective affluent future cried out for a massive celebration of our newfound wealth. With trembling hearts and hands, we withdrew half our cherished nest egg from the bank and bought orchestra seats for a hit Broadway show. Until now we could only afford cheap student tickets in the last two rows of the balcony, and joked that someday, in the far distant future, we might be rich enough to afford seats in the orchestra with Republicans. I had never seen one in the Bronx, but looking around, they didn't seem different from us, just older and better dressed. Before the show, we had an outrageously expensive dinner with champagne, and finished the evening with drinks at a nightclub.

We stumbled home on the subway, made love, and dreamed all night of our bright new future. We woke up with serious hangovers, and spender's regret about blowing so much of our safety net. There was also a niggling worry. The chair assured me the job was mine, but we had to wait for official approval from a college committee. It was just a formality; the committee always rubber stamped the department's and dean's decisions. He promised to call me as soon as it did.

I believed him, but neither Judy nor I could rest till we heard the final authorization. We didn't leave the house the next three days, just sat by the telephone in our underwear, too nervous to get dressed or even wash our faces. We brusquely cut off all callers, afraid the phone would be busy when the chair called. By the time we finally received the longed-for official good news, too drained to feel anything, even relief, we fell asleep on the floor. When we woke up, we celebrated again by throwing out the symbolic badges of our poverty: my gray parka and Judy's black winter coat. They were both misshapen and worn threadbare, but we couldn't afford to replace them until now.

The end of July 1961 marked the end of ten hard years for our family; like so many immigrants before and since, we had struggled to survive and succeed in our new country. We didn't find gold in the streets. There were no easy pickings, but after ten years we had carved out, each in his/her own way, a niche we could call our own. My brother was in elementary school but eventually got a Ph.D. in Mathematics. Dad, even though he didn't believe it, finally had a secure job that employed his talents. My mother developed several more or less legal and savory businesses in the United States and Israel. She later expanded to Argentina and Paraguay. I earned my union card, a Ph.D. in chemistry, and became, at least for a while, a college teacher. Maybe we weren't Yehnkees yet, but we weren't clueless greenhorns anymore either. We had become Americans in more than name only and felt safe and comfortable enough to burn our return tickets to the past.

ACKNOWLEDGEMENTS

I wrote this memoir for my children, born in the safety of America who at worst experienced only subtle, or even overt but nonlethal, forms of antisemitism. I wanted to introduce them to a tradition, and an extended family they never knew because its members were murdered by a regime and individuals fed by centuries of festering hate.

I had dreamed of becoming a writer since my days as a child, hiding from the Nazis in a root cellar. My parents taught me to read, and the few books my mother smuggled in broke down the walls of our dark, damp, oppressive prison. My body was constrained, but the stories I read freed my mind to roam limitless, exciting worlds. I couldn't think of anything more wonderful or worthwhile than writing stories which would similarly transport others. Through the years I thought it a fantasy, as realistic as hitting a homerun to win the seventh game in the World Series.

I am grateful to the many friends who read this memoir, asked permission to pass it on to their friends, and encouraged me to keep writing. I particularly want to thank my Carpinteria writers group. I joined them hesitantly years ago during our yearly escape from Philadelphia's harsh winters, hoping they wouldn't be too dismissive of a rank amateur. They not only accepted me into their ranks but became wonderful friends. Their thoughtful critique changed and shaped my writing. Recently I joined the St Peter's writers group in Philadelphia which is equally invaluable to my growth as a writer.

Several of my short stories were published in literary magazines, but I am grateful to Shawn Casselberry who after reading my memoir offered to publish it, proving that dreams can come through.

Finally, I want to thank my family; my wife Susan, my children, Lisa, Dan, Rachel, Hallie, and Marc and Kim who are unfortunately not with us anymore, for their love and support. They are the best part of my life.